HIKE THE PARKS

SEQUOIA & KINGS CANYON
NATIONAL PARKS

D1603559

HIKE THE PARKS
BEST DAY HIKES, WALKS, AND SIGHTS

SEQUOIA & KINGS CANYON NATIONAL PARKS

SCOTT TURNER

MOUNTAINEERS BOOKS

For that one tiny sequoia sapling I met in Giant Forest.
May you tower over everything long after I'm gone.

MOUNTAINEERS BOOKS is dedicated
to the exploration, preservation, and enjoyment
of outdoor and wilderness areas.

1001 SW Klickitat Way, Suite 201, Seattle, WA 98134
800-553-4453, www.mountaineersbooks.org

Printed in Korea
Distributed in the United Kingdom by Cordee, www.cordee.co.uk

First edition, 2020

Copyeditor: Erin Cusick
Design and layout: Heidi Smets Graphic Design
Cartographer: Erin Greb Cartography
All photographs by the author unless credited otherwise
Cover photograph: *Giant sequoias tower overhead in Sequoia National Park.*
(Photo by istock/lucky-photographer)
Frontispiece: *Iconic views down-canyon toward the Sphinx (Route 40)*

Library of Congress Cataloging-in-Publication Data is on file at https://lccn
.loc.gov/2019040788

Mountaineers Books titles may be purchased for corporate, educational,
or other promotional sales, and our authors are available for a wide range of
events. For information on special discounts or booking an author, contact
our customer service at 800-553-4453 or mbooks@mountaineersbooks.org.

Printed on FSC®-certified materials

ISBN (paperback): 978-1-68051-154-3
ISBN (ebook): 978-1-68051-196-3

An independent nonprofit publisher since 1960

CONTENTS

WOLVERTON, LODGEPOLE, AND DORST CREEK

REDWOOD CANYON

GRANT GROVE

KINGS CANYON

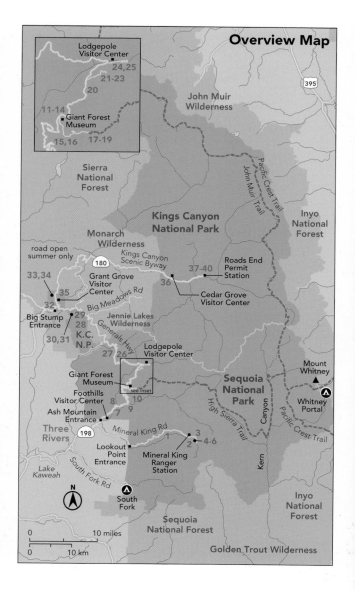

Overview Map

Inset (upper left):
- Lodgepole Visitor Center
- 24,25
- 21-23
- 20
- 11-14
- Giant Forest Museum
- 15,16
- 17-19

Main map:
- 395
- John Muir Wilderness
- Sierra National Forest
- John Muir Trail
- Pacific Crest Trail
- Kings Canyon National Park
- Inyo National Forest
- Monarch Wilderness
- road open summer only
- 180
- Kings Canyon Scenic Byway
- 33,34
- 35
- Grant Grove Visitor Center
- 37-40
- 36
- Roads End Permit Station
- Cedar Grove Visitor Center
- 32
- Big Meadows Rd
- Big Stump Entrance
- 29
- Jennie Lakes Wilderness
- 30,31
- K.C. N.P.
- Generals Hwy
- 28
- 27 26
- Lodgepole Visitor Center
- Giant Forest Museum
- see inset
- Mount Whitney
- Sequoia National Park
- High Sierra Trail
- Whitney Portal
- Foothills Visitor Center
- 8
- 10
- Ash Mountain Entrance
- 7
- 9
- Kern Canyon
- Pacific Crest Trail
- Three Rivers
- 198
- Mineral King Rd
- 1
- 3
- 2
- 4-6
- Lookout Point Entrance
- Mineral King Ranger Station
- Kern
- Lake Kaweah
- South Fork Rd
- South Fork
- N
- Sequoia National Forest
- Inyo National Forest
- Golden Trout Wilderness
- 0   10 miles
- 0   10 km

HIKES AT A GLANCE

HIKE	DISTANCE miles (km)	ELEVATION GAIN feet (m)	HIGH POINT feet (m)	DIFFICULTY
MINERAL KING				
1. East Fork Falls	3.4 (5.5)	800 (240)	6563 (2000)	Moderate
2. Cold Springs Nature Trail	2.3 (3.7)	500 (150)	7839 (2389)	Easy
3. Monarch Lakes	9.6 (15.4)	2600 (790)	10,627 (3239)	Challenging
4. Franklin Lake	11.4 (18.3)	2800 (850)	10,482 (3195)	Strenuous
5. White Chief Canyon	7 (11.3)	2200 (670)	10,046 (3062)	Challenging
6. Eagle Lake	6.8 (10.9)	2400 (730)	10,016 (3053)	Challenging
FOOTHILLS				
7. Potwisha Pictographs	0.8 (1.3)	150 (45)	2208 (673)	Easy
8. Marble Falls	6.4 (10.3)	1500 (460)	3613 (1101)	Challenging
9. Paradise Creek	5.6 (9)	1600 (490)	3851 (1174)	Challenging
10. Middle Fork Trail to Panther Creek	6.1 (9.8)	1200 (370)	3975 (1212)	Challenging
GIANT FOREST				
11. Beetle Rock	1.1 (1.8)	150 (45)	6455 (1967)	Easy
12. Sunset Rock	1.8 (2.9)	200 (60)	6455 (1967)	Easy
13. Round Meadow	1.3 (2.1)	100 (30)	6455 (1967)	Easy

OPPOSITE: *The General Sherman Tree dwarfs its human admirers (Route 20).*

HIKE	DISTANCE miles (km)	ELEVATION GAIN feet (m)	HIGH POINT feet (m)	DIFFICULTY
14. Soldiers Loop	4.2 (6.8)	800 (240)	6824 (2080)	Moderate
15. Moro Rock	0.5 (0.8)	300 (90)	6725 (2050)	Moderate
16. Sugar Pine Trail	3 (4.8)	700 (210)	6795 (2017)	Moderate
17. Circle Meadow	4 (6.4)	650 (200)	7118 (2170)	Moderate
18. Crescent and Log Meadows	2.1 (3.4)	200 (60)	6857 (2090)	Easy
19. Trail of the Sequoias	6 (9.7)	1200 (370)	7354 (2241)	Challenging
20. Congress Trail	2.8 (4.5)	500 (150)	7079 (2158)	Moderate
WOLVERTON, LODGEPOLE, AND DORST CREEK				
21. Wolverton to Giant Forest Museum	5.4 (8.7)	500 (150)	7233 (2205)	Moderate
22. Alta Peak	13.2 (21.2)	4200 (1280)	11,204 (3415)	Strenuous
23. Lakes Trail	12.2 (19.6)	2700 (820)	9567 (2916)	Strenuous
24. Tokopah Falls	3.8 (6.1)	600 (180)	7405 (2257)	Moderate
25. Twin Lakes	13.6 (21.9)	3000 (915)	9446 (2879)	Strenuous
26. Little Baldy	3.4 (5.5)	800 (240)	8044 (2452)	Moderate
27. Muir Grove	4.6 (7.4)	750 (230)	6869 (2094)	Moderate
REDWOOD CANYON				
28. Big Baldy Ridge	6 (9.7)	1700 (520)	8209 (2502)	Challenging
29. Buena Vista Peak	2 (3.2)	450 (140)	7605 (2318)	Easy

HIKE	DISTANCE miles (km)	ELEVATION GAIN feet (m)	HIGH POINT feet (m)	DIFFICULTY
30. Sugarbowl Loop	6.9 (11.1)	1400 (430)	6954 (2120)	Challenging
31. Hart Tree Loop	7.6 (12.2)	1500 (460)	6417 (1956)	Challenging
GRANT GROVE				
32. Big Stump Grove	1.3 (2.1)	250 (75)	6371 (1942)	Easy
33. Sunset Loop	6.3 (10.1)	1200 (370)	6572 (2003)	Challenging
34. Grant Grove	0.5 (0.8)	150 (45)	6411 (1954)	Easy
35. Park Ridge	5.6 (9)	1000 (300)	7772 (2369)	Challenging
KINGS CANYON				
36. Don Cecil Trail to Sheep Creek Falls	1.8 (2.9)	600 (180)	5190 (1582)	Moderate
37. Roaring River Falls	3.4 (5.5)	400 (120)	5023 (1531)	Moderate
38. Zumwalt Meadow	1.7 (2.7)	150 (45)	5051 (1540)	Easy
39. Kanawyers Loop	4.6 (7.4)	300 (90)	5157 (1572)	Moderate
40. Mist Falls	8 (12.9)	900 (270)	5857 (1785)	Challenging

VISITING SEQUOIA AND KINGS CANYON NATIONAL PARKS

At the moment you read this, snow-fed rivers pour over granite boulders within deep canyons, nourishing wildlife and flora spanning a bewildering range of habitats. The towering crown of a giant sequoia, survivor of fires and lightning strikes and witness to several millennia, sways gently in a west wind. A pristine lake nestled within a glacial basin shimmers in the crystalline high altitude. A determined hiker climbs toward a 12,000-foot (3658-m) mountain pass deep within the interior of the range. The hiker pulls deeply on the thin atmosphere while standing in awe of a vast panorama of mystifying size and scale.

These moments illustrate the hallmarks of Sequoia and Kings Canyon National Parks: size, variety, and the ability to impart lifelong memories. Both parks contain several groves of giant sequoias, largest of all trees by volume. Sequoia National Park contains the highest peak in the Lower 48—Mount Whitney—while Kings Canyon itself is one of the deepest canyons in the United States. Combined, the parks span an elevation range of nearly 13,500 feet (4115 m) from the summit of Mount Whitney to the Ash Mountain Entrance. Such superlative features ensure a sense of grandeur, along with one of the greatest displays of biodiversity in the country.

Although Sequoia and Kings Canyon National Parks are separate entities, the National Park Service manages both

OPPOSITE: *Ferns and falls compose a tranquil scene on the Hart Tree Loop (Route 31).*

parks conjointly. Combined, the two parks form one massive, sprawling mountain wonderland that also encompasses the northern unit of Giant Sequoia National Monument. Even though the combined parks contain over 800 miles (1287 km) of trail lacing through more than 860,000 acres (348,000 hectares) of mountainous terrain, most visitors explore the road-accessible destinations scattered along the parks' two main arteries: Generals Highway and CA Highway 180/Kings Canyon Scenic Byway.

Generals Highway begins at the Ash Mountain Entrance, east of Three Rivers, and threads a spectacular, winding ascent to the Giant Forest plateau. Generals Highway continues north through Lodgepole, Dorst Creek Campground, the Stony Creek Recreation Area, and access points to Giant Sequoia National Monument and the Jennie Lakes Wilderness before connecting with the Kings Canyon Scenic Byway just east of Kings Canyon National Park's Big Stump Entrance. After passing through Grant Grove, the byway descends into the depths of Kings Canyon before terminating at Roads End, a popular backcountry portal. A separate road covered within this guide, Mineral King Road, winds its way to Mineral King Valley, a subalpine mountain paradise boasting trails to several stunning lake basins.

GEOLOGY: THE RISE OF THE SIERRA NEVADA

The story of the Sierra Nevada begins with plate tectonics. Plate tectonics theory describes the earth's crust as a series of large moving plates that continually bump and grind against each other. This bumping and grinding shapes the surface of the earth by thrusting mountains upward, dragging valleys downward, and creating subterranean volcanic activity that creates the rocks that sometimes make their way to the earth's surface.

RISE UP, BATHOLITH!

Around one hundred to two hundred million years ago, the Pacific Plate began to slide underneath the North American Plate in a process known as subduction. As the subducted Pacific Plate sank and melted into the earth's mantle, a large pool of magma rose toward the surface and formed a large granitic mass, known as a batholith, about 10 miles (16.2 km) below the surface. Millions of years later, tectonic forces lifted the batholith toward the earth's surface. As the batholith rose, overlying metamorphic rock composed of ancient ocean sediments eroded. New watercourses carried the overlying rock westward, filling the Central Valley and exposing the underlying granite.

Within the last three million years, the Sierra Nevada batholith began to tilt, with the western edge of the range sinking and the eastern side of the range rising. The disproportionate tilt in the Sierra Nevada is evident when one views the range from both the Central Valley and the Owens Valley. From the Central Valley, one observes gently swelling foothills that rise to the conifer belt before culminating at the Great Western Divide. From the Owens Valley, one observes a severe, precipitous wall of granite known as an escarpment that steeply descends more than 8000 feet (2450 m) from the Sierra Crest down to the Owens Valley floor.

THE MICHELANGELO OF THE NATURAL WORLD

The Sierra Nevada's sculpted appearance is the result of extensive glacial activity during past ice ages. Slow-moving glaciers scoured rock out of preexisting depressions and canyons, sometimes peeling away huge volumes of land and leaving sheer cliff faces. Beneath the cliffs, U-shaped valleys, such as Kings Canyon and Kern Canyon, formed as the glaciers pushed through, clearing out massive quantities

Small pockets of ancient metamorphic rock cap the much younger granite of Big Baldy Ridge (Route 28).

of rock and carrying it down canyon. Smaller glaciers in the high country gouged out basins and valleys and sculpted the sharp pinnacles of the range's peaks. Many of these peaks still hold small, remnant glaciers and icefields on their northeast facing slopes, although that number continues to dwindle as the climate warms.

HUMAN HISTORY

Humans have inhabited the southern Sierra Nevada for up to seven thousand years. Various tribes of the Monache (or Western Mono) people inhabited flats along the five forks of the Kaweah River, while the Yokut people inhabited similar habitats around the Kings River watershed. Both peoples maintained seasonal villages in the foothills and higher elevations, and tribes traveled between the two throughout the year.

After European American prospectors discovered gold throughout the Sierra, opportunistic explorers flooded into the various canyons and valleys of the range. The first explorer of European origin to encounter the sequoias of Giant Forest was a man by the name of Hale Tharp. The Monache of Buck-eye Flat helped treat Tharp's companion for injuries at what is now known as Hospital Rock, and Monache guides later led Tharp to Giant Forest, where Tharp would eventually establish a seasonal cattle ranch at Log Meadow before ultimately becoming an advocate for protecting the sequoias. Although Tharp's influence in advocating protection was vital for the parks' future, his arrival ultimately heralded the decline and exodus of the indigenous peoples in the area.

Word about the trees quickly got out, and Bay Area lumbermen, already familiar with the exceptional timber provided by coast redwoods, set their sights on the sequoia groves as a means of satisfying San Francisco's insatiable desire for construction material. Within a matter of decades, the more accessible groves in the Kings River watershed—including the Converse Basin Grove—fell victim to wholesale logging operations. At the same time, the Kaweah Colony, a socialist utopian experiment set on funding their livelihood with sequoia timber, began constructing the old Colony Mill Road from the North Fork Kaweah River to the Giant Forest plateau. Ironically, sequoia timber is uniquely unsuitable for construction, owing to the brittle composition of the wood. When felled, sequoias shatter on impact, leaving only about 25 percent of the tree suitable for timber. And even that wood was suitable for little more than shingles, grapevine stakes, and perhaps most tragic of all, toothpicks.

An unlikely alliance of conservation efforts—spearheaded by John Muir—and agricultural interests concerned about the agricultural impacts of logging successfully petitioned Congress to create federal protections for the Grant Grove area and Giant Forest, and in 1890, President Benjamin Harrison signed legislation establishing Sequoia National Park and Grant Grove National Park. The legislation shut out the Kaweah Colony, which abandoned its efforts to complete the Colony Mill Road near present-day Crystal Cave Road.

US Army Cavalry troops were tasked with protecting the parks, but after several years of inconsistent and unfocused efforts, command was transferred to Colonel Charles Young, the third African American graduate of West Point. Young would become a formative figure in Sequoia's early history after completing the Colony Mill Road project and opening up Giant Forest to wheeled transportation for the first time. Over time, Colony Mill Road proved to be insufficient for increasing automobile traffic, and by 1926, the newly minted National Park Service had completed the Generals Highway, which would later extend north to connect with the Kings Canyon Scenic Byway in 1935.

Meanwhile, the ever-thirsty metropolis of Los Angeles had set its sights on obtaining water from the Kings River, which engineers considered ideal for water storage and

The Monache used these bedrock mortars to grind acorns and seeds (Route 21).

hydroelectric power potential. The plan was to establish a series of reservoirs within Kings Canyon and Tehipite Valley to store water for use by the city. After a furious battle between Southern California water interests and the ultimately victorious environmental lobby, Congress created legislation to combine Kings Canyon and most of its rugged watershed with Grant Grove National Park and a newly acquired parcel containing the Redwood Mountain Groves to form a new Kings Canyon National Park in 1940. Because it abuts Sequoia National Park along the Kings-Kaweah and Kings-Kern Divides, the National Park Service manages both parks conjointly as one massive mountain park.

The parks' growing pains led to a recognition that more would need to be done to protect the sequoia groves than prevent fires. In fact, the parks realized that suppressing fire was detrimental, which gave rise to the practice of controlled burns. Additionally, the parks gradually removed visitor services within the sequoia groves to less sensitive adjacent sites, leaving the intact sequoia groves at Grant Grove, Giant Forest, and Redwood Canyon in relatively pristine condition.

FLORA AND FAUNA

Thanks to a wide elevation range that exceeds 13,000 feet (3962 m), Sequoia and Kings Canyon National Parks harbor an astonishing diversity of plant and animal life. Rising crown and branches above the rest, the mighty sequoia dominates the flora scheme with species ranging from minute to massive, providing some of the parks' greatest highlights.

FLORA

Sequoias. Despite inhabiting a relatively trivial amount of acreage throughout the parks and adjacent national forests and monuments, sequoias occupy a place of honor among the Sierra Nevada's flora. With a size unparalleled anywhere, aside from the sequoia's taller but thinner cousin, the coast redwood, the giant sequoia both impresses and bewilders visitors with its magnificence.

Sequoias grow rapidly and achieve impressive statures in a relatively short time. As observed at previously logged groves, such as Atwell Grove and Big Stump Grove, 120-year-old sequoias can tower over older white firs and sugar pines. The trees reach full height quickly, while the remainder of their growth occurs as the trees attain girth as they age (much like adult humans). Sequoias continue to grow until they become so large that their root systems can no longer support their weight. The number one cause of death among sequoias is toppling.

Sequoias can reach heights exceeding 270 feet (82 m), thicknesses of up to 40 feet (12 m) at the base, and weights exceeding thousands of tons. While other trees exceed the sequoia in terms of height (coast redwood and Douglas fir), age (bristlecone pines), and diameter (tule cypress), no other tree occupies as much sheer volume as a sequoia. Even the tree's branches, many of which are the size of mature conifers, tell the tale of the tree's massiveness. The lower branches of the Sherman Tree are larger than any single tree east of the Mississippi River.

Sequoias, unlike most other conifers, are uniquely well adapted to periodic wildfires. The tree's fibrous, cinnamon-colored bark can be several feet thick and contains fire-resistant tannins—tannins that are resistant even to the hottest, most destructive fires and that also serve to repel termites and other wood-consuming insects, such as bark beetles. Sequoias also depend on fire for reproduction. Like most members of the cypress family, sequoia cones open and release their seeds in response to heat. During fires, sequoia cones open, showering the now bare forest floor with oat-sized seeds. Following a fire, countless sequoia saplings will sprout from the ground. North Grove, which burned during

OPPOSITE: *Fire-resistant sequoias may have burn scars, but the flames rarely kill them.*

the 2015 Rough Fire, displayed countless saplings a mere eight months following the massive conflagration.

PRESCRIBED BURNING

In the early 1960s, park foresters began to recognize that sequoias were not reproducing as expected. Before receiving federal protection, fires rolled through sequoia groves, clearing out competing vegetation and setting the stage for regeneration. Fire suppression, therefore, eliminated the ability of the tree to regenerate while creating clusters of smaller trees, which allowed fires to climb into the sequoias' crowns. Today, the parks set periodic controlled fires to clear out the competing understory and allow the sequoia to regenerate. Most controlled burns occur during the early summer over a small area, usually about 150 acres (60 hectares).

Chaparral. Chaparral, a low-growing scrub and shrub community, tends to occupy sunny, south-facing slopes in the lower elevations. Most chaparral species have evolved tough, leathery foliage that maximizes the plants' ability to retain moisture. Principal species within chaparral communities include chamise, ceanothus (lilac), manzanita, scrub oak, flannel bush, and a number of flowering vines and annual flowers.

Oak Woodland. Woodlands are low-density forests often of nonconiferous trees that proliferate throughout the foothills. As elevation increases, the species composition changes. Lower elevation woodlands feature open stands of deciduous blue oaks, interior live oaks, and California buckeye. At higher elevations, from 2500 feet (760 m) to 4000 feet (1220 m), canyon live oaks and California bay laurel replace blue, live, and valley oaks. Above 4000 feet, conifers and the deciduous black oak begin to appear among everdenser woodlands of broadleaf evergreens.

Riparian Woodland. The word *riparian* means "water loving," and plants within this community depend on reliable sources of water to survive. In the foothills, you will find sycamores, maples, alders, cottonwoods, and willows forming dense gallery forests with a thriving understory of lush ferns, herbs, and flowers. Within the yellow pine forest, watercourses and meadows support black cottonwood, willows, and occasional groves of quaking aspens. In the red fir–lodgepole belt and subalpine habitats, larger groves of quaking aspen join black cottonwood along watercourses, particularly in meadows. The foliage of the quaking aspen, which gets its name for the leaves' tendency to shimmer in the slightest breeze, changes into a variety of brilliant colors during early autumn.

Mixed-Conifer Forest. The western Sierra Nevada contains two distinct bands of mixed-conifer forest: the yellow pine belt (also known as lower montane forest), which thrives

A tiger swallowtail sampling nectar from a Western wallflower

between 5000 feet (1500 m) and about 7500 feet (2290 m), and the red fir–lodgepole belt (also known as upper montane forest), which blankets the elevations from 7500 feet (2290 m) to 9500 feet (2900 m). These forest belts take their names from the predominant tree species. Yellow pine refers to a class of pines that includes ponderosa pines in lower elevations and Jeffrey pines in higher elevations. The yellow pine belt also includes white firs, sugar pines, incense cedars, black oaks, and sequoias. Red fir and lodgepole pines characterize the higher belt, although you will also find Western junipers, Western white pines, and Jeffrey pines. The two conifer belts receive the greatest amounts of precipitation in the parks, with the yellow pine belt averaging between 30 and 45 inches (75 and 115 cm) annually and the red fir–lodgepole belt averaging between 60 and 90 inches (150 and 230 cm) annually.

Meadows. Meadows tend to occur in depressions bounded by granitic masses. Water flowing through these depressions creates marsh conditions where trees cannot grow. A rich mixture of grasses creates brilliant-green open spaces dotted by a wide variety of wildflowers. Given this mixture of succulent vegetation, meadows tend to attract more wildlife than any other part of the forest. Visit a meadow early in the morning or early in the evening, and you stand a good chance of spotting deer, black bears, and other forest creatures.

Subalpine and Alpine Habitat. As the elevation increases, temperatures grow colder to a point most conifers cannot tolerate. Shorter growing seasons and lingering snow packs tend to reduce understory plants to grasses and wildflowers. The subalpine zone, a narrower coniferous belt ranging from about 9500 feet (2900 m) to the tree line at 10,500 to 11,000 feet (3200 to 3350 m), features conifers of dwindling size and density, including Western white pines, lodgepole pines, and ancient foxtail pines that live for up to three thousand years.

At tree line, most trees become little more than shrubs that often grow in a prostrated form known as *krummholz*, until they disappear entirely at the boundary of icy alpine habitats that lie beneath snow for most of the year.

A CHANGING CLIMATE

Beginning in 2012, the state of California experienced its worst drought in over a thousand years. Most climate scientists correlate the intensity of this drought with the exacerbating effects of climate change, which for California can be summed up in two words: *warmer* and *drier*. A corresponding rise in average temperatures has reduced the amount of precipitation that falls as snow, which in turn has led to a reduced snowpack. As a result, the conifer belt has begun to experience an unprecedented die-off. Between 2010 and 2018, ecologists estimate that over 130 million conifers succumbed to drought-related causes and bark beetle infestations through the central and southern Sierra Nevada. Consistent rises in temperatures coupled with diminished snowpacks in the future suggest that the sequoia groves and the great western Sierra conifer belt face an uncertain future, especially as uncontrollable summer wildfires become the new normal across the West.

FAUNA

The vast forests of the western Sierra Nevada shelter a wide array of wildlife, ranging from seldom-seen salamanders to an active population of black bears. Hikers, particularly early birds, have a good chance of experiencing this diverse spectrum of fauna as they explore the trails.

Mammals. The western Sierra Nevada hosts a variety of mammals—seventy-two total species to be exact. Included within this tally are mule deer, yellow-bellied marmots, ground and tree squirrels, chipmunks, martens, pikas, foxes, bobcats, a variety of bats, and a variety of other rodents. In

A juvenile black bear pauses during his evening buffet.

addition, the two largest mammals, and easily the two animals that cause visitors the most concern, are the California black bear and the mountain lion. Both animals can be found throughout the range and at most elevations, although hikers are very unlikely to encounter mountain lions. This guide includes pertinent safety information on both animals in the Safety section.

Reptiles. Herpetology fanatics will find plenty to enjoy in the Sequoia and Kings Canyon regions. Visitors may encounter a variety of venomous and nonvenomous snakes throughout the park, including common species such as rattlesnakes (see the Safety section for more on these guys), gopher snakes, garter snakes, racers, and king snakes. Of these snakes, few are more beautiful than the California mountain king snake. Mountain king snakes have a distinctive tricolor pattern of red, black, and white that often arranges in bands. A number of small lizards scamper about on rocks and bask in the sun, especially in the foothills and lower elevation forests.

Amphibians. Among the region's local frogs, the Sierra Nevada yellow-legged frog and the southern yellow-legged frog populations have declined by as much as 90 percent over the last hundred years. Much of this decline occurred as a result of the introduction of non-native trout species, which feast on the eggs and tadpoles that the frog lays in sunny areas of ponds, creeks, and lakes. Wherever non-native trout have been removed, frog populations have rebounded. The endemic Sequoia salamander lives primarily within the Kaweah watershed between elevations of 1600 feet (490 m) and 7200 feet (2190 m) in coniferous forests and riparian woodlands. This species is critically imperiled. The other amphibian that you might see is the Sierra newt. Shaped much like a lizard, but infinitely cuter, these red critters crawl slowly while camouflaged along the forest floor in damp areas, so watch where you put your feet in those habitats.

Birds. Over two hundred species of birds reside throughout both parks and the adjacent national forests. Look up into the sky during your explorations of the foothill areas, and it's likely that you will see any number of large raptors soaring in circles high above, gliding along on the thermals and scouring the ground for any sign of movement. The most commonly sighted raptors in the park are the hawks, including red-tailed hawks, red-shouldered hawks, northern goshawks, Cooper's hawk, and the migratory Swainson's hawk.

Far larger and more dramatic are the range's two resident eagle species, the bald eagle and the golden eagle, two human-averse species that occupy old conifer snags adjacent to watercourses or lakes. The Sierra Nevada also hosts several different species of owls. Owls are seldom seen by most hikers since they prefer to hunt from dusk until dawn. Invisible though they may seem to humans, it is not uncommon to hear owls hooting throughout the night. Small burrowing owls inhabit the former burrows of ground squirrels in open grassy areas throughout the foothills.

The *Corvidae* genus includes crows, ravens, jays, and nutcrackers. Crows and their larger cousins, ravens, are clever birds with long memories and are often found around inhabited areas. Picnickers in the parks are likely to encounter the Steller's jay. This jay's beautiful blue plumage invites initial interest, but turn your back for a second, and these ill-mannered birds are likely to steal whatever snack you were about to eat.

Another avian curiosity found within the red fir–lodgepole belt is the grouse. This large, blue-mottled bird uses its color to camouflage itself on the forest floor. Male grouses create a deep, booming noise that can carry for up to a mile or so.

MUST-SEE SIGHTS AND ACTIVITIES

Both parks feature a number of memorable highlights, only some of which include hiking. Be sure to save some time in your itinerary for a few of these must-see attractions.

HOSPITAL ROCK

The first white man to explore the region we now call Sequoia National Park, Hale Tharp, encountered the indigenous Monache near this location. The Monache treated Tharp's friend for an injury next to the large pictograph panel just north of Buckeye Flat Road. This beautiful foothill destination features a picnic area, a short access trail that reaches the Middle Fork Kaweah River, and several other native features in addition to Hospital Rock itself.

CRYSTAL CAVE

The Sequoia and Kings Canyon frontcountry is littered with caves caused by eons of erosion that gouged out softer metamorphic rocks. Crystal Cave is one of only two that are open for visitation, the other being Boyden Cave in Sequoia National Forest. Reservations can be made online at www.recreation.gov, and you can obtain your ticket at the trailhead for the short path that descends nearly 400 feet (122 m) to the mouth of Crystal Cave. Several options for exploring

The President stands as the third tallest sequoia in the world (Route 21).

the cave range from a short, family-friendly tour to a half-day spelunking adventure.

GIANT FOREST MUSEUM
The Giant Forest Museum provides an overview of climate, history, natural history, and area trails, with friendly rangers

and staff available to answer your questions. The Giant Forest Museum also features a shuttle terminus with three different Sequoia Shuttle routes: Green Route 1 between the museum and Lodgepole, Gray Route 2 between the museum and Crescent Meadow, and the Visalia Route (Blue) that runs from Visalia to Giant Forest. Multiple trailheads radiate from the museum and adjacent parking area, making this an important hub for Giant Forest exploration.

MORO ROCK

Sequoia National Park's signature exfoliation dome swells from the southwest edge of the Giant Forest plateau for a commanding view of the Great Western Divide and Middle Fork Kaweah River canyon. A masterful bit of engineering produced a winding staircase that leads to the summit.

Zumwalt Meadow's lush vegetation is a haven for wildlife (Route 38).

Sunsets from the top are phenomenal affairs, but be sure to avoid Moro Rock during thunderstorms or when the staircase is icy to avoid potentially fatal experiments with lightning bolts and rapid, gravity-assisted descents.

CRESCENT MEADOW
Called the "gem of the Sierra" by none other than John Muir, this sprawling meadow is another focal point for hiking in Giant Forest. Several trails, including the historic High Sierra Trail, begin here, as does a spider's web of footpaths that encircle Crescent Meadow and nearby Log, Huckleberry, and Circle Meadows. A picnic area and a shuttle stop add to the convenience of this essential Giant Forest destination.

GENERAL SHERMAN TREE AND THE CONGRESS TRAIL
This is the one destination that every visitor to Giant Forest must see, and for good reason. No single-stemmed organism on the planet is as large as the General Sherman Tree, and that alone is worth a bit of wandering. Combine your pilgrimage to General Sherman with a loop on the nearby Congress Trail. The Congress Trail visits several other impressive sequoias, including the President, the House, Senate, and Founders Group, and several other notable trees named after American historic figures.

REDWOOD CANYON
Considered to be the area with the largest concentration of sequoias in the world, the complex of groves within Redwood Canyon is also one of the best preserved. A network of trails explores the groves, which are at their loveliest in late spring, when thickets of mountain dogwoods blossom and Redwood Creek rumbles along through a corridor of towering sequoias. Even a short stroll along the Sugarbowl, Hart Tree, or Redwood Canyon Trails yields a wealth of beautiful sights and sounds. The nearby Kings Canyon Overlook and

Redwood Canyon Overlook offer roadside stops that take in impressive vistas.

GENERAL GRANT TREE

This towering sequoia tree is the second-largest sequoia on the planet, and it is also the namesake tree of a small but beautiful grove of sequoias. The short loop that visits the tree and its attendant historical and arboreal highlights is easy enough for everybody, even toddlers. Fun fact: the General Grant Tree is the "nation's Christmas tree," and the park has held a ceremony at the base of the tree since President Calvin Coolidge formalized the tree's honorary distinction in 1926.

PANORAMIC VIEW

Although there are viewpoints peppered throughout the Grant Grove and Hume Lake area, none encompass as impressive a view as Panoramic View on the north end of Park Ridge. Park Ridge itself is no stranger to impressive views. The Forest Service and Park Service jointly operate a forest-fire lookout on the ridge's southern end, and the Park Ridge Trail has some of the best vistas in the parks. The easy, paved trail to the point makes this spot accessible to everybody. Come at sunrise to watch the rising sun transcend the fabled Kings Canyon high country.

ZUMWALT MEADOW

This can't-miss destination in the heart of Kings Canyon is accessible by way of a short, easy looping hike. The sprawling meadow soaks in water from the nearby South Fork Kings River, attracting wildlife (and mosquitoes) like a magnet. Visit during the morning when wildlife are at their most active, and you may spot an array of songbirds, mule deer, and black bears foraging in the meadow.

KEY STATISTICS

Sequoia National Park

- Established: September 25, 1890
- Acreage: 404,064 acres (163,519 hectares)
- Low point: Ash Mountain Entrance (1700 feet [520 meters])
- High point: Mount Whitney (14,505 feet [4421 meters])
- Average annual visitation: 1.2 million

Kings Canyon National Park

- Established: October 1, 1890 (General Grant National Park); March 4, 1940 (Kings Canyon National Park)
- Acreage: 461,901 acres (186,925 hectares)
- Low point: Kings River, west of Cedar Grove (4491 feet [1369 meters])
- High point: North Palisade (14,248 feet [4343 meters])
- Average annual visitation: 700,000
- Combined designated wilderness: 93 percent (808,000 acres [327,000 hectares])

PLANNING YOUR TRIP

Sequoia National Park features a wealth of facilities that cater to your needs within seven primary hubs of activity described in each chapter. Each of these hubs contains additional services, which in the case of Lodgepole, Grant Grove, and Kings Canyon also include lodges, markets, dining, campgrounds, and post offices.

THE SEQUOIA SHUTTLE

The Lodgepole–Giant Forest region offers a convenient, free shuttle system, with four different lines connecting the area's trailhead and campgrounds. The Green Line connects the Giant Forest Museum and Lodgepole with stops at the Sherman Tree Accessible Parking Area and the General Sherman Tree Parking Area. The Orange Line travels between the Sherman Tree Accessible Parking Area and Wolverton, with a stop at the General Sherman Tree Parking Area. The Gray Line travels from the Giant Forest Museum to Crescent Meadow, with a stop at Moro Rock. The Purple Line travels from Lodgepole to Dorst Creek, with a stop at Wuksachi Lodge. An additional shuttle (Blue), available for a fee and through reservation only, travels between the town of Visalia and the Giant Forest Museum.

VISITOR CENTERS

Before you set out on the trails, it's always a good idea to stop by the visitor center adjacent to the area you'll be

OPPOSITE: *Good luck turning your back on the jaw-dropping view at Pear Lake (Route 23).*

hiking. Rangers can provide information on trail conditions, and you can also pick up overnight permits, souvenirs, and get some education on local flora and fauna.

Mineral King Ranger Station: Located at Mile 24, Mineral King Road, Three Rivers, CA 93271, across from Cold Springs Campground. The station's season varies according to when the snowpack melts enough to reach the station and when the first snow falls. Open daily, from 8:00 AM to 4:00 PM. Phone: 559-565-3768.

Foothills Visitor Center: Located at 47050 Generals Highway, Three Rivers, CA 93271, 1 mile (1.6 km) from the Ash Mountain Entrance. Open daily, from 8:00 AM to 4:30 PM. Hours vary in winter. Phone: 559-565-3341.

Giant Forest Museum: Located on Generals Highway, 16.4 miles (26.4 km) from the Ash Mountain Entrance. Open daily, from 9:00 AM to 4:30 PM. Hours vary in winter. Phone: 559-565-3341.

Lodgepole Visitor Center: Located at 63100 Lodgepole Road, Sequoia National Park, CA 93262. Open hours vary according to season. Phone: 559-565-4436.

Kings Canyon Visitor Center: Located at 83918 CA Highway 180, Kings Canyon National Park, CA 93633. Open daily, from 8:00 AM to 5:00 PM. Hours vary according to season. Phone: 559-565-3341.

Cedar Grove Visitor Center: Located at North Side Drive, Cedar Grove, CA 93633 (next to Sentinel Campground). Open daily, from 9:00 AM to 5:00 PM mid-May to mid-October. Phone: 559-565-3793.

Roads End Permit Station: Located at the end of CA Highway 180, Cedar Grove, CA 93633. Open daily, from 7:00 AM to 3:00 PM mid-May to mid-October. Phone: 559-565-3341.

CAMPING AND LODGING

Both parks and the adjacent Giant Sequoia National Monument feature a wealth of different camping and lodging options. This overview lists only some of the campgrounds and lodges along Generals Highway and CA Highway 180/ Kings Canyon Scenic Byway.

FOOTHILLS

Potwisha Campground is located on Generals Highway, 3.7 miles (6 km) east from the Ash Mountain Entrance, and is open year round. The campground features 42 reservable campsites, flush toilets, drinking water, food storage lockers, ADA accessibility, and an RV dump station.

Buckeye Flat Campground is located on Buckeye Flat Road, 6.7 miles (10.8 km) east from the Ash Mountain Entrance. The campground is open from mid-March to late September. The campground features 28 campsites, flush toilets, food storage lockers, and drinking water.

GIANT FOREST/LODGEPOLE AREA

Lodgepole Campground is located on Generals Highway, 20.9 miles (33.6 km) east from the Ash Mountain Entrance. The campground is open year round. Lodgepole Campground features 214 campsites, flush toilets, drinking water, food storage lockers, and an RV dump station. The nearby village of Lodgepole features a visitor center, market, restaurants, a post office, and a nearby picnic area.

Wuksachi Lodge is located on Wuksachi Way, 22.4 miles (36 km) east and north from the Ash Mountain Entrance. This is Sequoia's only lodge, and in many ways it rivals the great lodges of Yosemite. Wuksachi Lodge features 102 rooms, a full-service restaurant, a cocktail lounge, a retail shop that's open year round, and special event facilities.

Dorst Creek Campground is located on Generals Highway, 29 miles (46.7 km) north from the Ash Mountain Entrance. The campground is open from mid-June through September. The campground features 218 campsites, 4 of which are group campsites, as well as ADA-accessible sites, flush toilets, an RV dump station, food storage lockers, and a water station.

GIANT SEQUOIA NATIONAL MONUMENT

Lower and Upper Stony Creek Campgrounds are located on Generals Highway, 13.7 miles (22 km) south from Kings Canyon National Park's Big Stump Entrance. Both campgrounds are open from early June to mid-September. The lower campground features 50 sites, and the upper campground has 24 sites. The lower campground is more developed with flush toilets, drinking water, and food storage lockers. The upper campground has pit toilets, drinking water, and food storage lockers, but also boasts a quieter ambiance.

The small, rustic **Stony Creek Lodge** offers 11 rooms just up the road from the two Stony Creek campgrounds and a reasonable drive away from Grant Grove, Giant Forest, and the Big Meadows Trailheads. The lodge is open only from May through mid-October due to the tendency of heavy snowfall to close Generals Highway between Grant Grove and Giant Forest.

The **Montecito Sequoia Lodge**, on Generals Highway 4.3 miles (7 km) north of Stony Creek Lodge, features an array of activities year round, including winter activities such as cross-country skiing and snowshoeing. The property contains a private lake, a year-round hot tub, and a variety of seasonal activities that go far beyond hiking. The lodge also offers an all-inclusive Summer Adventure Camp that include meals, lodging, and a variety of activities catering to all age ranges.

GRANT GROVE

Sunset Campground is located on CA Highway 180, 2.9 miles (4.7 km) north from the Big Stump Entrance and is open from late spring to late summer. The campground contains 157 campsites and 2 large group sites available by reservation. Amenities include flush toilets, drinking water, pay phones,

Yellow-bellied marmots have attitude to spare.

and food storage lockers. The nearby Grant Grove Village area also features a visitor center, a market, and a restaurant.

Azalea Campground is located on CA 180, 3.4 miles (5.5 km) north from the Big Stump Entrance, and is open year round. The campground contains 110 campsites available on a first-come, first-served basis. Amenities include flush toilets, drinking water, and food storage lockers. The nearby Grant Grove Village area also features a visitor center, a market, and a restaurant.

Crystal Springs Campground is located off of CA 180, 3.4 miles (5.5 km) north from the Big Stump Entrance and then heading east on the road to Panoramic View. The campground contains 36 individual sites and 14 medium-sized group sites available by reservation between late spring and early fall. Amenities include flush toilets, drinking water, and food storage lockers. The nearby Grant Grove Village area also features a visitor center, a market, and a restaurant.

The **John Muir Lodge** provides the most comfort and luxury of all sleeping options within the parks. Built in 1998, Grant Grove's primary lodging option features 36 rooms, Wi-Fi, and an adjacent restaurant within its rustic confines on the north end of Grant Grove Village.

The **Grant Grove Cabins** offer a compromise between the luxury of the Muir Lodge and car camping. A nice variety of cabins ranging from the largest duplex cabins down to more intimate hybridized tent cabins runs the gamut of options. Visitors with a taste for history can choose the Honeymoon Cabin (#9), a historic building erected in 1910 that remains the oldest structure still standing in the park.

KINGS CANYON

Sheep Creek Campground is located on CA 180, 31.5 miles (50.7 km) east from the Big Stump Entrance. The campground contains 111 campsites available on a first-come, first-served basis and is open between early spring and late fall. Amenities include flush toilets, drinking water, and food storage lockers. Nearby Cedar Grove also has a market, a restaurant, showers, a visitor center, and laundry.

Sentinel Campground is located on North Side Drive across from the Cedar Grove Lodge, 31.9 miles (51.3 km) east from the Big Stump Entrance via CA 180. The campground contains 82 campsites available on a first-come, first-served basis and is open between early spring and late fall. Amenities include flush toilets, drinking water, and food storage lockers. Nearby Cedar Grove also has a market, a restaurant, showers, a visitor center, and laundry.

Canyon View Group Campground is located on CA 180, 32.4 miles (52.1 km) east from the Big Stump Entrance. The campground contains 12 group campsites available on a first-come, first-served basis and is open between late spring and early fall. Amenities include flush toilets, drinking water, and food storage lockers. Nearby Cedar Grove also has a market, a restaurant, showers, a visitor center, and laundry.

Moraine Campground is located on CA 180, 32.7 miles (52.6 km) east from the Big Stump Entrance. The campground contains 121 campsites available on a first-come, first-served basis and is open from late June to early September.

Amenities include flush toilets, drinking water, and food storage lockers. Nearby Cedar Grove also has a market, a restaurant, showers, a visitor center, and laundry.

The **Cedar Grove Lodge** is Kings Canyon's answer to those who don't want to sleep on the ground. This rustic lodge stands near the rest of Cedar Grove's facilities, including the market, restaurant, laundry, showers, and visitor center.

WHEN TO VISIT

Both parks are open year round, although some parts of the park, including Mineral King Valley and Kings Canyon, close during the winter. Weather is a primary consideration for best times, as a deep snowpack often blankets the high elevations between November and May, although a network of snowshoeing routes provide access to the Giant Forest area. Conversely, prodigious summer heat makes hiking below 5000 feet (1500 m) uncomfortable and dangerous.

VISITING THE PARKS IN WINTER

Wintertime brings a dense snowpack to the higher elevations, which cuts off access to a lot of high-country destinations. Mineral King Valley closes entirely between late October and late spring, as does Kings Canyon. Although Giant Forest, the Foothills, Lodgepole, and Grant Grove remain open except during heavy snowfall, the Generals Highway may close between them, and chains may be required at any time. Several of the hiking routes within Giant Forest and Lodgepole are marked for snowshoeing by a yellow triangle emblazoned with a symbol denoting a specific trail. While snowshoeing a given route, look for these triangles about 8 to 10 feet (2.5 to 3 m) up on trees along the route. The Lodgepole Visitor Center sells a map specifically highlighting the snowshoeing routes.

When covered with snow, Crescent Meadow Road doubles as a snowshoeing route (Route 18).

WEATHER AND CLIMATE

Mild, sunny summers and cold, snowy winters characterize the climate of the Sierra Nevada. The shoulder seasons of spring and fall feature more variable weather, which can vacillate between mild and sunny, and cold and snowy. The peak of the wet season occurs between December and March, with most of the region's precipitation falling during this time. The higher elevation of the Sierra Nevada receives the majority of its precipitation in the form of snow, while elevations below 5000 feet (1500 m) receive most of the precipitation as rain. Sporadic precipitation in the shoulder seasons (October–November and April–May) provides a less significant amount of rain and snow, while summer storm activity provides a mostly trivial amount of precipitation despite its dramatic delivery.

The higher elevations of the Sierra are famous for creating their own weather. The range's legendary summer storms appear seemingly out of nowhere, with the sudden ominous rumble striking apprehension into the hearts of alpine hikers. Always exercise caution when hiking in the higher elevations after noon, as the weather can change suddenly and dangerously. It's wise to start early for high-altitude hikes.

PARK PERMITS AND REGULATIONS

Any trip to Sequoia and Kings Canyon will benefit from an awareness of the regulations created to protect the parks, their habitats, and their resident wildlife. Please keep these rules in mind as you explore.

DAY-USE AREAS

In order to curb overuse, many of the road-accessible destinations covered in this guide are managed as day-use areas. This is particularly true of the Giant Forest area, which is still recovering from decades of overuse that caused significant damage to the grove. This guide indicates which hikes are open only to day use and which hikes are open to backcountry camping.

BACKCOUNTRY CAMPING

A number of the hiking routes in this guide can double as overnight backpacking trips. Hikers seeking to camp in Sequoia and Kings Canyon backcountry must first obtain a permit. Between mid-September and mid-May, hikers can obtain walk-up permits for all of the backcountry trailheads in the parks. During the busiest months (mid-May to mid-September), the parks manage permits through a quota system, although a limited number of walk-up permits remain available.

Owing to the popularity of some routes described within this book (Alta Trail, High Sierra Trail, Twin Lakes,

Bubbs Creek, and Woods Creek in particular), reserving a permit via the parks' reservation system is crucial to successfully obtaining one. To do so, visit www.nps.gov/seki /planyourvisit/wilderness_permits.htm. From here, you can download the Wilderness Permit Application and email it to the parks' wilderness permit reservations system. You can reserve permits up to two weeks in advance.

Rangers will approve (or deny) your permit based on availability, and they will inform you of the results via email. Once you have the reservation confirmed, you must pick up the permit from the relevant wilderness permit office located within the visitor center or ranger station located closest to the specific trailhead you want to start from. At that time, rangers will give you a run-down on safety and etiquette as well as answer any questions about conditions along the route.

FOOD STORAGE

Sequoia and Kings Canyon National Parks host an active population of California black bears. Black bears love our

Eagle View on the High Sierra Trail reveals the Sequoia high country (Route 19).

calorie-dense foods, and they will gladly relieve you of your snacks if you give them an opportunity. It is both your responsibility and a legal imperative that you store all of your food and any other scented items (this includes sundries and toiletries) inside provided food storage lockers found at campgrounds and at trailheads. In the backcountry, store your food in an approved storage container.

TRAIL USE

Avoid shortcutting trails. Shortcutting trails results in an increase in erosion that damages the tread of the trail. Cairns, or ducks, are piles of rocks that are usually stacked in order to mark nonmaintained routes. Some cairns have stood for decades, and they have been placed by rangers specifically to guide hikers. Refrain from knocking them over. Conversely, creating new cairns adds confusion and is considered a form of graffiti.

DOGS

As wonderful as it can be to have your four-legged friends along with you, dogs are not allowed on trails within either park. Dogs are allowed on roads so long as they are leashed, and they are also welcome within campgrounds and picnic areas. Keep in mind that dogs pose a threat to wildlife, and given the park's mandate to protect the flora and fauna within it, wildlife gets priority.

FIREARMS

Federal law allows people who can legally possess firearms to possess them within the park according to state laws and regulations. Firearms are not permitted in certain facilities, and those facilities always display signs indicating firearm restrictions.

DRONES

Drones are remote-operated, unmanned aircraft that people use for videography or simply for fun. However, the park forbids the use of drones to limit noise pollution, protect habitats and wildlife, and preserve scenic and wilderness values.

WILDLIFE

Day-use areas exist in part to protect wildlife, as many mountain species are most active at night. The parks also expect that you will avoid feeding, handling, or pestering park wildlife so as to minimize disruption to their daily activities. Every year, visitors receive injuries because they feed wildlife, which causes wildlife to become aggressive. (See the Safety section below for more information on encountering specific animals.)

CAMPFIRES

Within the lower elevations, campfires are permitted only within designated campfire rings. In some backcountry areas below 9000 feet (2740 m) in Sequoia National Park and 10,000 feet (3050 m) in Kings Canyon National Park, you may have a small fire in established campfire rings. The parks may issue prohibitions on campfires at any time when the weather favors wildfire development.

SAFETY AND OUTDOOR ETIQUETTE

The following sections break down the various safety and trail etiquette considerations that you'll need to prepare for in order to ensure that you'll have a safe, responsible visit to the parks. Although hiking in the Sierra carries with it a number of risks, following these recommendations will protect you from most adverse situations.

HAZARDS

The habitats of Sequoia and Kings Canyon present a number of challenges and safety concerns to hikers. Brush up on some safety knowledge here to ensure a safe and satisfying series of adventures.

Altitude. Altitude sickness is the body's negative response to reduced oxygen at high altitudes. Symptoms include lack of appetite, nausea, vomiting, headaches, lethargy, dizziness, swelling in the hands and face, insomnia, shortness of breath, the sensation of pins and needles, drowsiness, excessive flatulence, unsteady gait, dry cough, and general malaise. If you begin to feel any of these symptoms, retreat to a lower elevation immediately. Continuing to ascend under these conditions will exacerbate the symptoms. Adequate hydration can help stave off some of the symptoms. Acclimation, a process whereby hikers gain altitude slowly and over several days before attempting to hike at high and very high altitudes, is the best way to prevent altitude sickness.

Heat. The parks, especially at the lower elevations, can become dangerously hot, and those conditions can result in heat cramps, heat exhaustion, and heatstroke. Heat cramping may occur in the abdomen, leg muscles, and arm muscles. Heat exhaustion occurs during prolonged exposure to high temperatures and is often accompanied by dehydration. Symptoms include thirst, weakness, headaches, and loss of consciousness. Heatstroke, the body's failure to regulate internal temperatures, can cause catastrophic or fatal damage. Avoid cooking your internal organs by staying hydrated, staying off the trails if it's warmer than 85 degrees Fahrenheit (29.5 Celsius), and staying off the trails between 11:00 AM and 5:00 PM on days when the forecast calls for hot weather.

Cold. The Sierra can also become dangerously cold, especially at high altitude, during winter, during the shoulder seasons of spring and fall, and whenever a hiker becomes wet during cooler conditions. If you plan on hiking in temperatures below 50 degrees Fahrenheit (10 Celsius), prepare for the cold by wearing layers. Being able to add or

Pear and Emerald Lakes viewed from Alta Peak (Route 22)

subtract layers as you go allows you more flexibility to cope with temperature fluctuations. Think of the three W's: wicking, warmth, and weather. Your base layer should be a synthetic layer that wicks moisture. The middle layer(s) should be warmer, such as a fleece pullover. The final layer can be a relatively thin material that blocks out rain and wind.

Sun Exposure. The atmosphere at higher elevations is thinner than at lower elevations, and a thinner atmosphere allows more UV radiation through. Carry adequate sun protection in the form of sunscreen, and reapply the sunscreen every two hours. Wide-brim hats keep the sun off of the face and neck. Sunglasses can block the UV rays from scorching your sensitive retinas. Light-colored, loose-fitting clothes can help to reflect some of the sunshine away, whereas dark-colored clothing absorbs heat. Hikers may even consider carrying a reflective umbrella to repel the worst of the sun's fury on long, exposed hikes.

Thunderstorms. The Sierra Nevada is prone to sudden thunderstorms, especially during the summer. These storms can develop rapidly, and the risk of electrocution by lightning can be high if you are hiking at exposed higher elevations. If you see clouds beginning to build up, retreat toward shelter immediately. Your safest bet for avoiding electrocution is to study the weather reports and avoid hiking in exposed areas during the afternoon when thunderstorms are most common.

Snowmelt. Every winter, most areas of the Sierra receive copious amounts of snow. During the spring, this snow begins to melt, and the melted snow—commonly known as water—courses down canyons, ravines, and streams with alarming ferocity. The best time to cross creeks is during the early morning, when potentially melting snow at higher elevations is still frozen. However, if you are trying to cross a major creek during peak snowmelt, it may not be safe no matter what time. Consult with rangers ahead of time if your route calls for unimproved creek crossings.

Giardia. Giardia, a nasty little microorganism found in most of the parks' watercourses, settles into the intestines and stomach and produces giardiasis. Symptoms include severe diarrhea, dehydration, gas, cramping, nausea, vomiting, and spectacular crash dieting. There are a variety of water-purification methods available to hikers, including boiling water, using chemicals to sterilize the water, using ultraviolet radiation to sterilize water, and filtering water through a ceramic filter by way of suction. Boiling is the most effective method (at least 1 to 3 minutes), but it is also time consuming and requires fuel. Each of the methods have their disadvantages, but it's better than spending the next several weeks on the toilet.

PLANT AND WILDLIFE CONCERNS

If it's not the environment that's testing your mettle, it's the flora and fauna. While most plants and animals in the Sierra are benign, the following concerns present issues ranging from mild nuisance to considerable, but avoidable danger.

Poison Oak. This deciduous vine favors shady areas and is often associated with the understory of oak trees. The leaves, stems, and stalk of the plant contain an oil that acts as a skin irritant and produces a rash that may persist for weeks. When scratched, the oil may spread across the body, resulting in rashes that occur in a variety of places, each seemingly more uncomfortable than the last. Poison oak does not grow above 5000 feet (1500 m), so it is primarily a foothill phenomenon. Hikers can avoid it by learning to recognize it by sight (*Leaves of three . . .*) and therefore carefully avoiding it (*. . . let it be*). If exposed, wash the affected area with soap and water immediately. Soap will help to remove the oil. Water will only spread it around.

Ticks. These bloodsucking parasites lie in wait at the edges of branches of lower and middle elevation flora and latch on to passing warm-blooded animals. When they bite, they burrow their heads and suck your blood. In their twisted, sick idea of a fair trade, the tick leaves behind toxins and bacteria.

Perform periodic tick checks as you hike to remove any hitchhikers. If a tick does manage to sink its pincers into your skin, use a pair of pliers (this is where multi-tools come in handy) and grip the tick as close to the head as possible. Pull steadily but firmly, making sure to pull the head directly from your body. Clean the wound thoroughly and often, as infections can occur. A small percentage of ticks carry Lyme disease (although primarily in midwestern and northeastern states), a bacterial infection with flu-like symptoms. Antibiotics can curb Lyme disease before it causes too much damage. If you have been bitten by a tick, and especially if it has been embedded for several days, your best course of action is to consult your physician as soon as possible.

Mosquitoes. The scourge of the backcountry voyager favors marshes, meadows, lakes, and any other places where standing water can accumulate. They are most active during the cooler periods of the day (dawn and evening), although they may be present at any time. Mosquitoes will sink their proboscis into your skin, suck your blood until they become engorged, and leave painful, itchy bumps that will drive you mad for several days. DEET, an insecticide, effectively deters mosquitoes even if it is probably one of the last things you want to slather all over yourself. A second option is permethrin, another insecticide that you can use to treat your clothing.

Rattlesnakes. Rattlesnake venom can destroy skin tissue, blood cells, and cause internal hemorrhaging. Rattlesnakes inhabit the foothills and lower elevations of the mixed-conifer forests, although they can be found as high as 10,000 feet (3050 m). Rattlesnakes do not seek out humans to attack as they are shy, retiring creatures that dread encountering you far more than you dread encountering them. If you are bitten, seek medical attention immediately. If you are in the backcountry, know where the nearest ranger stations are; they can provide assistance.

Marmots. Marmots are accomplished food thieves, especially at the higher elevations. In Mineral King Valley, marmots appear to have cultivated a taste for radiator hoses, particularly during the spring and early summer. The critters nestle into engine compartments and start gnawing on cables and hoses. When hikers return from their excursions, their cars fail to start, stranding them an extraordinary distance from civilization. Wrapping cars to protect the undercarriage using large tarps and bungee cables has become all the rage at Mineral King. The method denies access to marmots and gives you an opportunity for a comical prehike portrait with your diapered automobile.

Black Bears. Black bears are retiring, vaguely comical creatures who, despite their fearsome appearance, try to

When your car needs a marmot diaper

stay away from humans. Unlike grizzly bears, they are usually not aggressive, and most black bears will climb a tree if they perceive a threat from humans. Generally speaking, all you need to do to avoid an unpleasant encounter with a bear while on the trail is to give them as wide a berth as possible. Given that bears are most interested in calorie-dense foods, protecting your food against bears goes a long way toward protecting yourself against bears. Always follow food storage rules, and you will minimize the possibility of a negative bear encounter. Although black bears are unlikely to display aggression, should you experience a dangerous situation with a bear, wave your arms, slowly back away, avoid eye contact, and speak in a nonthreatening voice. If the bear won't budge, make larger movements with your arms and make a lot of noise. If attacked (very rare), fight back and concentrate on hitting the bear's face and muzzle. Do not run, no matter what.

Mountain Lions. Mountain lions are a large apex predator that primarily hunt other mammals, especially deer. They are shy, reclusive, and mostly nocturnal, which means that most hikers will never see one. Hikers who set out before dawn or continue past dusk have a slightly higher chance of encountering them. If you do meet a mountain lion, face it down and make a ton of noise. Appear as large as possible and do not run. Fleeing may trigger a predatory response that convinces the cat that you're food. If attacked, fight back. Report any sightings or incidents with mountain lions to the rangers immediately.

NAVIGATION

Dense forests can challenge even the most highly developed navigational skills. Some of the trail networks described here are confusing, especially to those who aren't already familiar with the routes. GPS devices can become unreliable due to the tree cover, leaving the good old-fashioned map and compass as your most reliable means of finding where you are.

THE TEN ESSENTIALS

The Ten Essentials, originated by The Mountaineers, are particular items necessary to answer two crucial questions: Can you prevent emergencies and respond positively should one occur? And can you safely spend a night—or more—outside? This list is a starting point to guide you in preparation for your Sequoia and Kings Canyon adventure.

1. **Navigation:** The five fundamentals are a map, altimeter, compass, GPS device, and a personal locator beacon or other device to contact emergency first responders. Note that cell phone applications can provide the first four features, but those applications are known to fail.

2. **Headlamp:** A light source other than your smartphone will help you find your way in darkness should you run out of daylight. Include spare batteries.

3. **Sun protection:** Wear sunglasses, sun-protective clothes, and broad-spectrum sunscreen rated at least SPF 30.

4. **First aid:** Basics include bandages; skin closures; gauze pads and dressings; roller bandage or wrap; tape; antiseptic; blister prevention and treatment supplies; nitrile gloves; tweezers; needle; nonprescription painkillers; anti-inflammatory, anti-diarrheal, and antihistamine tablets; topical antibiotic; and any important personal prescriptions, including an EpiPen if you have severe allergies.

5. **Knife:** Also consider a multi-tool, strong tape, some cordage, and gear repair supplies.

6. **Fire:** Carry at least one butane lighter (or waterproof matches) and a firestarter, such as chemical heat tabs, cotton balls soaked in petroleum jelly, or a commercially prepared firestarter.

7. **Shelter:** In addition to a rain shell, carry a single-use bivvy sack, plastic tube tent, or jumbo plastic trash bag.

8. **Extra food:** For shorter trips, a one-day supply is reasonable.

9. **Extra water:** Carry sufficient water and have the skills and tools required to obtain and purify additional water.

10. **Extra clothes:** Pack additional layers needed to survive the night in the worst conditions that your party may realistically encounter.

OUTDOOR ETIQUETTE

In order to become a positive rather than negative influence on park habitats, begin by learning, reviewing, and thoroughly internalizing the seven Leave No Trace principles. These principles are the basis for understanding how to enjoy outdoor spaces responsibly.

Plan Ahead and Prepare. Prior to setting out on your hike, take some time to learn the specific restrictions and regulations related to the area you wish to explore. Weather, terrain, and animal behavior in the Sierra can be unpredictable; prepare for emergencies accordingly. Ensure that the terrain you are traveling on and the distances you are planning to cover are within your and everybody in your group's ability. Be sure to carry the appropriate amount of clothing, food, water, and gear for the route you are taking; this includes bringing basic essentials.

Travel and Camp on Durable Surfaces. Vegetation in the Sierra, particularly in the high country, is delicate, sensitive, and very slow to recover from trampling. Never camp on vegetation. Select only durable surfaces, and seek out established campsites where possible. Camp at least 25 feet (8 m) away from water and more than 100 feet (30 m) if terrain permits. Do not add "improvements," including campfire rings, rock walls to screen wind, or cairns (rock piles), to campsites. Rangers regularly maintain existing campfire rings, and they do a fine job without your help.

Dispose of Waste Properly. Most people, especially on their initial wilderness excursions, are mildly to moderately disturbed about the likelihood of having to poop without being able to magically vanish said poop by pushing of a lever. In the wilderness, when you are taking the Browns to the Super Bowl, bury your waste at least 6 to 8 inches deep. Bring a trowel to make the job easier. You *must* pack out all toilet paper. Toilet paper takes a long time to biodegrade, and it has a nasty way of working its way back up to the surface. Also be sure to pack out every other bit of trash you bring with you. Never use any kind of soap, no matter how "environmentally sensitive" it is, within a water supply. Wash at least 100 feet (30 m) away from streams, rivers, and lakes.

Leave What You Find. It may seem perfectly innocent to collect a pine cone or pick up a stick. However, that pine cone and that stick are part of the habitat. Even if they look like they are not doing anything to further the future of the wilderness, they too have a role in the wild. By removing natural objects from the wilderness, you are harming the wilderness. This also applies to cultural artifacts. The artifacts are part of the cultural heritage of indigenous and pioneering peoples. They are also part of the historical record. Moving or removing any cultural artifact diminishes our cultural heritage and our wilderness experience, not to mention it's aganst the law.

Minimize Campfire Impacts. Generally speaking, it is better to forego fires in the wilderness. (See Park Permits and Regulations for specific campfire restrictions.) If you insist on building a fire, use existing campfire rings. Keep the fire small. Always attend to the fire so that it doesn't grow out of control and burn the forest down. Completely extinguish all fires by drowning them with water and stirring until they are no longer warm. Do not burn your trash. Melting plastic releases toxins, and aluminum foil will not burn.

Respect Wildlife. Feeding wildlife alters their natural behaviors and can either expose them to predators or cause them to become aggressive. Most bear aggression occurs because they get a taste for human food. When denied human food afterward, they go to extraordinary lengths to get it. Ultimately, rangers must step in and kill aggressive bears that have been fed by humans. Observe all wildlife from a distance for their safety and yours. Always store your food appropriately and as directed by park regulations. Always refrain from feeding wildlife.

Be Considerate of Other Visitors. It should go without saying that you are not the only one trying to enjoy your trip, but your respect goes a long way toward protecting the experience of everybody. Show courtesy. Yield to others on the trail. Allow other people space when camping and when taking breaks. Keep your voice down in order to let natural

SUGGESTED ITINERARIES + 57

sounds prevail. This last principle also applies to playing music through speakers as you hike, as many hikers find this a distraction and disruption to their enjoyment of the habitat.

SUGGESTED ITINERARIES

The three itineraries here present a one-day option for each park as well as a three-day option that takes in the highlights of both parks.

ONE DAY: SEQUOIA NATIONAL PARK

This single day of exploration focuses almost exclusively on hikes within the Giant Forest, which features some of the region's best hiking, views, and notable natural curiosities.

- Hospital Rock: a well-preserved pictograph panel next to a picnic area and staircase descending to the Kaweah River.
- Giant Forest Museum: a fine introduction to the Giant Forest's history and ecosystems.
- Crescent Meadow (Route 18): stop by the "gem of the Sierra" for picnicking or a short hike.
- General Sherman and the Congress Trail (Route 20): the signature trail of the Giant Forest area, with stops at the largest single-stem tree on the planet.
- Sunset from Beetle Rock (Route 11), Sunset Rock (Route 12), Hanging Rock (Route 14), or Moro Rock (Route 15): nothing beats those fiery San Joaquin Valley sunsets, and all four of these spots offer great viewpoints.

ONE DAY: KINGS CANYON NATIONAL PARK

A single day of exploration at Kings Canyon is somewhat challenging owing to the amount of driving that's involved. However, this itinerary fitted into a very long day captures most of the best highlights.

- Big Stump Grove (Route 32): a dose of logging history and a pleasant hike through tranquil meadows.

- General Grant Grove (Route 34): visit the second-largest sequoia in its namesake grove.
- Panoramic Point: outstanding views across the Hume Lake area and beyond to the Kings Canyon high country.
- Roaring River Falls (Route 37): Kings Canyon's noisiest and most accessible waterfall.
- Zumwalt Meadow (Route 38): a peaceful, family-friendly hike full of water, wildlife, and dramatic scenery.

THREE DAYS: SEQUOIA AND KINGS CANYON NATIONAL PARKS

At the bare minimum, three days gives you enough time to see the most popular features of both parks while carving out a bit of extra time to enjoy some additional exploration. Each day is divided up to allow one moderate morning hike, a short afternoon adventure with a visit to a museum or other nonhiking destination, followed by a short evening hike to take advantage of the southern Sierra's beautiful sunsets.

Day One: Sequoia National Park
- Hospital Rock Picnic Area: a well-preserved pictograph panel next to a picnic area and staircase descending to the Kaweah River.
- Trail of the Sequoias (Route 19): the most comprehensive and secluded route through the Giant Forest.
- Giant Forest Museum: a fine introduction to the Giant Forest's history and ecosystems.
- Crescent Meadow (Route 18): stop by the "gem of the Sierra" for picnicking or a short hike.

Day Two: Sequoia National Park
- Tokopah Falls (Route 24): Sequoia's largest and most dramatic waterfall.
- Crystal Cave: a series of caves carved into subterranean marble in the Sequoia foothills.

Pictographs at Hospital Rock testify to the area's importance to the indigenous Monache

- General Sherman and the Congress Trail (Route 20): the signature trail of the Giant Forest area, with stops at the largest single-stem tree on the planet.
- Travel to General Grant Grove: not only does this give you a full day in Kings Canyon on day three, but the Generals Highway is a destination unto itself.

Day Three: Kings Canyon National Park

- Park Ridge (Route 35): this route includes Panoramic Point, and it's one of the most satisfying in the Grant Grove area.
- General Grant Grove (Route 34): don't miss the chance to say a quick hello to the world's second-largest sequoia.
- Zumwalt Meadow (Route 38): a peaceful, family-friendly hike full of water, wildlife, and dramatic scenery.

HOW TO USE THIS GUIDE

The collection of routes included in this book captures a variety of hiking experiences, including short nature trails, casual walks to historical sites, moderate summit ascents, rambling explorations of fantastic geologic features, satisfying half-day hikes that sample a variety of highlights, and a few challenging hikes to notable park high points and lakes that can double as overnight routes.

GEOGRAPHIC REGIONS

This guide breaks down the park into seven geographic regions, listed in the following order: Mineral King Valley; the Foothills; Giant Forest; Wolverton, Lodgepole, and Dorst Creek; Redwood Canyon; Grant Grove; and Kings Canyon. The first four chapters cover various regions of Sequoia National Park's western half, while the last three chapters cover Kings Canyon National Park's western half.

The Generals Highway connects the Foothills region, beginning from the Ash Mountain Entrance east of Three Rivers, to the junction of Generals Highway and CA Highway 180/Kings Canyon Scenic Byway. CA 180 runs west to east from the Big Stump Entrance to Roads End in Kings Canyon, and the majority of the Kings Canyon destinations, except for Redwood Canyon, are located here. Mineral King Road stands aloof from those two main arteries and is the only driving route into and out of Mineral King Valley.

OPPOSITE: *The sparkling, translucent waters of the Kings River (Route 39)*

KEY HIKE INFORMATION

Each hike begins with the following information to help you get a good handle on key characteristics of the route.

DISTANCE, ELEVATION GAIN, AND HIGH POINT

This information refers to the distance a hike covers and the amount of elevation gain. Note that this guide displays cumulative elevation gain, as opposed to calculating the difference between the lowest and highest points on a hike. This gives hikers a better idea of how much climbing is in store. This section also includes the elevation of the high point for the route. All values are listed in both the English and metric systems.

All distances, elevation gain, and high points were derived from GPS data collected during field work and extrapolated through Caltopo.com. All distances and elevations except for high points are rounded up. Please note that due to the inherent variability of GPS data, your mileage may vary slightly from what's presented here.

DIFFICULTY AND TRAIL SURFACE

Each hike is categorized into one of four separate ratings for difficulty: easy, moderate, challenging, and strenuous. These ratings are calibrated toward the mythical "average hiker," who maintains a reasonable degree of fitness and has at least some hiking experience. Bear in mind that many hikers fall on either side of average. Please understand that your fitness level and experience may skew these ratings. Conditions on trails vary dramatically throughout the parks; these details are covered in the trail surface section.

Easy: Short, family-friendly hikes that nearly all hikers can finish comfortably. Approximately 0.4–3 miles (0.6–4.8 km) and up to 300 feet (90 m) of elevation gain.

Moderate: Longer hikes that most reasonably fit hikers can complete in two to four hours. Approximately 2.5–7 miles (4–11.3 km) and up to 850 feet (260 m) of elevation gain.

Challenging: Half-day hikes suitable for experienced hikers that may also contain some cross-country navigation, difficult terrain, and steep slopes. Approximately 5–9 miles (8–14.5 km) and up to 1500 feet (460 m) of elevation gain.

Strenuous: Full-day hikes suitable for experienced, well-conditioned hikers that contain cross-country navigation, difficult terrain, and steep slopes. Approximately 8–14.2 miles (12.9–22.9 km) and up to 4200 feet (1280 m) of elevation gain.

MAPS

The maps section references the appropriate USGS topographic map to refer to for routefinding. Given the nature of mountain travel, which often includes travel through dense forests that can scramble a person's directional orientation, it is *highly recommended* that hikers use a topographic map and a compass on routes that call for routefinding.

You can purchase USGS topo maps directly from www.usgs.gov/products/maps/topo-maps. The website https://caltopo.com is a phenomenal online resource that, among

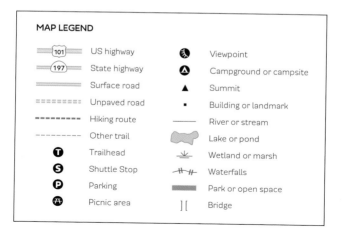

MAP LEGEND

US highway	Viewpoint
State highway	Campground or campsite
Surface road	Summit
Unpaved road	Building or landmark
Hiking route	River or stream
Other trail	Lake or pond
Trailhead	Wetland or marsh
Shuttle Stop	Waterfalls
Parking	Park or open space
Picnic area	Bridge

many other things, allows you to customize topographic maps specifically for the hike you wish to take. You can also purchase a high-quality trail map depicting Giant Forest from the Lodgepole Visitor Center.

GPS COORDINATES

This section provides GPS coordinates for the location of each trailhead. Coordinates are listed in decimal degrees (based on the WGS84 datum), as that's the easiest way to enter the coordinates into websites and mapping applications.

NOTES

The notes section includes specific information related to terrain, navigation, whether a hike is open to day use or overnight use, whether there's a restroom or toilet at the trailhead, whether the trail has interpretive features, or any other unique quality that merits mention.

HIKE DESCRIPTIONS

A brief description of each trail provides an overview of what you can expect to find on the hike, including notable features, specific challenges, or other features unique to each route.

GETTING THERE

Driving directions begin from the nearest park entrance. For hikes in Mineral King Valley, directions are reckoned from the junction of North Fork Road and CA Highway 198 in downtown Three Rivers, and from that point the directions lead to Mineral King Road. For hikes within the Foothills; Giant Forest; and Wolverton, Lodgepole, and Dorst Creek regions, the Ash Mountain Entrance east of Three Rivers is the starting point. For hikes within Redwood Canyon, Grant Grove, and Kings Canyon, the Big Stump Entrance east of Fresno and Squaw Valley on CA Highway 180 is the starting point.

The **Transit** section provides information based on the available Sequoia Shuttle that services the busier sections of the park (Giant Forest, Lodgepole) where applicable.

ON THE TRAIL

This section contains the turn-by-turn directions and other notable features you'll need to know in order to complete and enjoy the hikes.

Going Farther refers to additional directions that allow you to extend your route to nearby destinations. In some cases, this refers to alternate return routes or approaches.

A NOTE ABOUT SAFETY

Safety is an important concern in all outdoor activities. No guidebook can alert you to every hazard or anticipate the limitations of every reader. Therefore, the descriptions of roads, trails, routes, and natural features in this book are not representations that a particular place or excursion will be safe for your party. When you follow any of the routes described in this book, you assume responsibility for your own safety. Under normal conditions, such excursions require the usual attention to traffic, road and trail conditions, weather, terrain, the capabilities of your party, and other factors. Keeping informed on current conditions and exercising common sense are the keys to a safe, enjoyable outing.

—*Mountaineers Books*

MINERAL KING VALLEY

Mineral King has followed a rough and rocky road on its path toward inclusion into the national park system. The valley has witnessed mining booms and busts, a devastating earthquake, and a proposal from Walt Disney that nearly turned the valley into a ski resort. Having ridden all those waves, nobody can say that Mineral King is without its blemishes and scars. But even after all the human activity here, the valley remains a mountain lover's paradise.

Mineral King features two small first-come, first-served campgrounds (Atwell Mill and Cold Springs), several trailheads, and a ranger station that offers the only services in the valley. This modest amount of services coupled with a long drive on a winding, badly maintained road ensures that Mineral King has a quieter ambiance than the rest of Sequoia's frontcountry.

One unique caution applies to Mineral King. A lively population of yellow-bellied marmots reside within the valley. Every spring, the marmots emerge from winter slumbers, and occasionally they make a meal out of radiator hoses and other crucial engine components. Legends tell of marmots hitching rides inside engine compartments all the way back to civilization. Hikers have taken to wrapping the undercarriages of their cars in huge tarps strapped together with bungee cables—imagine a massive blue diaper, and you get the idea. Unless you want to pay a tow-truck company, come prepared to deal with the marmots.

OPPOSITE: *The Franklin Pass Trail leading to the heart of Mineral King Valley (Route 4)*

1   EAST FORK FALLS

Distance: 3.4 miles (5.5 km)
Elevation gain: 800 feet (240 m)
High point: 6563 feet (2000 m)
Difficulty: Moderate
Trail surface: Dirt
Map: USGS 7.5-min Silver City
GPS: 36.464438°, -118.667179°
Notes: Day use only; good for kids; toilets located within Atwell Mill Campground

> A picturesque cascading waterfall is your reward for following the opening stretch of the Atwell-Hockett Trail on a moderate descent to the banks of the East Fork Kaweah River. A rustic wooden bridge spans the river just below the falls, and several sequoias tower above a leafy riparian canopy of alders. This route visits both Atwell Grove and East Fork Grove, with the former grove offering a lesson on the resilience of sequoias.

GETTING THERE

From North Fork Drive in downtown Three Rivers, drive east for 3.8 miles (6.1 km) on CA Highway 198, and turn right onto Mineral King Road. Follow the winding, poorly maintained road for 19.3 miles (31 km) to Atwell Mill Campground. Turn right to enter the campground, and find parking in the dirt lot just outside the campground entrance. The Atwell-Hockett Trailhead lies on the west end of the campground, about 0.2 mile (0.3 km) from the parking area.

ON THE TRAIL

Unless you're camping at Atwell Mill Campground, you will start your hike by walking west through the campground. The formal Atwell-Hockett Trailhead lies on the west side of the campground near a grassy meadow that's littered with

Bridge over the East Fork Kaweah River

the debris of the old millworks from the days when a logging operation attempted to exploit the Atwell Grove's sequoias. A lot of the sequoias in the lower part of the grove were chopped down, and you'll see numerous stumps on your way through the campground. Many of the grove's younger sequoias were saplings around the time the grove was logged, and less than one hundred years later, those trees already tower above the surrounding conifers.

After passing the meadow, the trail bends to the left and descends toward the East Fork Kaweah River. The sequoias disappear as you enter a south-facing slope graced with Jeffrey pines and incense cedar rising from a fragrant ground cover of bear's clover. A few sequoias cluster around the banks of Deadwood Creek at the 1-mile (1.6-km) mark. After dipping in and out of that drainage, the trail makes its final descent toward a picturesque wooden bridge that spans the East Fork Kaweah River just below a cascading waterfall.

The falls thunder along just east of the bridge. During the early-season snowmelt (May through June), a prodigious amount of water courses over the falls as Mineral King's snowmelt feeds the East Fork. During the latter half of summer and into fall, the falls become much quieter. Evening is a

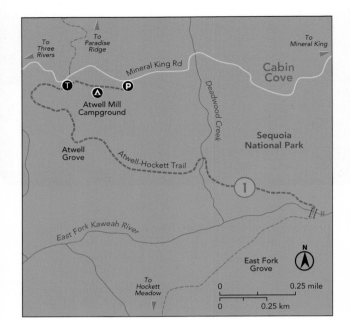

nice time to enjoy the scene, especially when the sinking sun's light casts an appealing glow on the lush foliage surrounding the falls. A handful of sequoias along the riverbank herald the beginning of East Fork Grove, which extends southwest along the Atwell-Hockett Trail for another 2 miles (3.2 km).

GOING FARTHER

You can continue along the Atwell-Hockett Trail for another 2 miles (3.2 km) to explore a bit more of East Fork Grove. For a much more involved route, you could follow the Atwell-Hockett Trail all the way to Hockett Meadow, where you'll find some peaceful backcountry camping alongside the spacious meadow. The roundtrip hike to Hockett Meadow (21.4 miles/34.4 km with 4500 feet/1371 m of elevation gain) is strenuous, and it is best enjoyed as an overnight hike.

2 COLD SPRINGS NATURE TRAIL

Distance: 2.3 miles (3.7 km)
Elevation gain: 500 feet (150 m)
High point: 7839 feet (2389 m)
Difficulty: Easy
Trail surface: Dirt
Map: USGS 7.5-min Mineral King
GPS: 36.451436°, -118.610928°
Notes: Day use only, pit toilet available within Cold Springs
Campground

> Although the diminutive Cold Springs Nature Trail lacks the
> challenge and scale of other Mineral King trails, the family-
> friendly route along the East Fork Kaweah River trades
> difficulty for gentle beauty. With lush meadows, frequent
> wildlife sightings, and abundant wildflowers, this landscape
> will inspire everyone from experienced hikers to kids taking
> some of their first outdoor forays. Fall color enthusiasts
> will find brilliant displays in early October thanks to several
> quaking aspen groves along the route.

A view of Empire Mountain from the Cold Springs Nature Trail

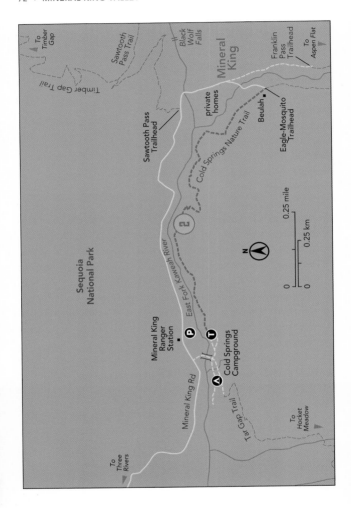

GETTING THERE

From North Fork Drive in downtown Three Rivers, head east for 3.8 miles (6.1 km) on CA Highway 198 to a junction with Mineral King Road. Turn right onto the narrow, twisting, and occasionally unpaved Mineral King Road and make your slow and careful way east for another 23.4 miles (37.7 km) to Cold Springs Campground and the Mineral King Ranger Station. You'll find parking directly across from the ranger station. Walk back along the road into the campground, and keep left after the bridge. The trailhead is next to campsite 6.

ON THE TRAIL

Follow the trail east from campsite 6 into a lush meadow studded with aspens, red fir, and lodgepole pines. For the next 0.8 mile (1.3 km), you will follow the course of the East Fork Kaweah River while climbing at a gentle grade. Tree-framed views of Timber Gap, Empire Mountain, and Sawtooth Peak contrast with the intimate shimmering of aspen leaves, carpets of wildflowers, and the trickle of icy springs underfoot.

At 0.8 mile (1.3 km), the trail passes through a meadow graced with the aromatic scent of Great Basin sagebrush before bending south into Mineral King Valley. A small cluster of cabins, which predate the inclusion of Mineral King into Sequoia National Park, lie ahead and on your left. These cabins stand on the site of a small mining town known as Beulah, which served as a processing center for minerals mined from the surrounding mountains. The Cold Springs Nature Trail ends at an access road servicing these cabins. This is your turnaround spot.

GOING FARTHER

For a great fall-color adventure, turn left before you reach the Eagle-Mosquito Trailhead and cross the bridge over the East Fork Kaweah River. Turn right to reach the Franklin Pass Trailhead. From there, you can continue along the Franklin Pass Trail for 1.1 miles (1.8 km) to Aspen Flat.

BEULAH

Beulah was once the epicenter of mining activity during Mineral King's short mining boom. The town prospered until the 1906 San Francisco earthquake sent an avalanche downhill, wiping out most of the structures. That effectively put an end to mining, but people continue to inhabit the Beulah site to the present day. The cabins you see here pre-date the inclusion of Mineral King into Sequoia National Park, and therefore the homeowners are allowed to maintain their properties. Please respect the property as you would your neighbor's home.

3   MONARCH LAKES

Distance: 9.6 miles (15.4 km)
Elevation gain: 2600 feet (790 m)
High point: 10,627 feet (3239 m)
Difficulty: Challenging
Trail surface: Dirt and rock
Map: USGS 7.5-min Mineral King
GPS: 36.453275°, -118.596751°
Notes: Suitable for backpacking; food storage lockers at Lower Monarch Lake; restroom at trailhead

The hike to Monarch Lakes is one of several starting in Mineral King that climb out of the valley and past the tree line to reach shimmering alpine lakes. Mineral King's unusual geology is on display from start to finish in the form of metamorphic rock outcrops that add color not usually found with the typical gray Sierra Nevada granite. Abundant campsites, a food storage locker, and a pit toilet with stellar views make the Monarch Lakes a fine place for an overnight excursion.

GETTING THERE

From downtown Three Rivers at the junction of North Fork Road and CA Highway 198, head east for 3.8 miles (6.1 km) to Mineral King Road, and turn right. Follow the narrow, twisting road for 23.4 miles (37.7 km) to the Mineral King Ranger Station. Continue beyond the ranger station for another 0.8 mile (1.3 km) to the Sawtooth Pass Trailhead parking area on the left side of the road. If you are hiking early in the season, be sure to wrap your vehicle in a tarp to protect it from marmots. (See the chapter overview for more details on these naughty little buggers.)

ON THE TRAIL

The beginning of the Sawtooth Pass Trail is breathtaking in both the figurative and literal senses. The scenery, which consists of verdant hillsides swelling to alpine summits, may have you channeling your inner Julie Andrews and belting out "The Sound of Music." However, you may have a hard time hitting the high notes since the initially steep grade will demand every oxygen molecule your lungs can suck up.

Over the first 0.25 mile (0.4 km), you pick up 300 feet (90 m) of elevation gain before the grade mellows out at the trail's first switchback. From that switchback, peer into the ravine on your right to see a spring spilling out of the rock to fuel cascading Monarch Creek. The trail then doubles back to the northwest, reaching a junction with the Timber Gap Trail at 0.6 mile (1 km). Keep right and begin a prolonged climb through a hillside dotted with junipers and Jeffrey pines rising from a fragrant carpet of Great Basin sagebrush (a.k.a. cowboy cologne). At 1.3 miles (2.1 km) the trail crosses Monarch Creek where it rumbles through a lush meadow carpeted with wildflowers during early summer.

After crossing Monarch Creek, the trail switchbacks up the southern wall of Monarch Creek's canyon through groves of

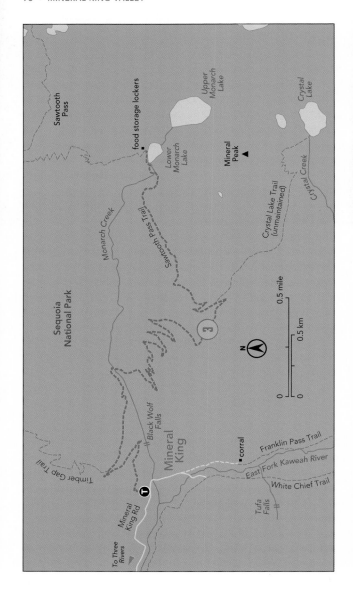

Lower Monarch Lake

red fir and Western white pine interspersed with spring-fed meadows. Views into Mineral King Valley improve considerably as you wrap around a ridge at 3 miles (4.8 km). The trail continues climbing past a junction with an unmaintained trail to Crystal Lake at 3.3 miles (5.3 km). From that junction, the trail switches back once again before passing a few foxtail pines heralding the approach of tree line at the 10,000-foot (3050-m) elevation mark.

The trail next begins a stunning traverse of a rocky hillside that may hold snow and ice into early summer. The lack of tree cover ensures unobstructed views of the stunning canyon before you. The canyon walls appear painted with dark reds and purples, and a patina of green vegetation hugging the banks of Monarch Creek in the canyon below creates a pleasing color scheme.

This beautiful traverse ends at 4.2 miles (6.8 km) as the trail dips into a basin just below Lower Monarch Lake to cross several rivulets and finally Monarch Creek for a final time. After the crossing, the trail hugs the creek as it makes one final climb to the base of Lower Monarch Lake at 4.5 miles

(7.2 km). The campsites, food storage lockers, and afore-mentioned pit toilet lie on the north side of the lower lake. The larger Upper Monarch Lake lies a short distance to the southeast from the lower lake. There's no formal trail, but you can reach it via a short, steep scramble over granite slabs.

4   FRANKLIN LAKE

Distance: 11.4 miles (18.3 km)
Elevation gain: 2800 feet (850 m)
High point: 10,482 feet (3195 m)
Difficulty: Strenuous
Trail surface: Dirt
Map: USGS 7.5-min Mineral King
GPS: 36.450515°, -118.595011°
Notes: Suitable for backpacking; food storage lockers at parking area for trailhead; pit toilet adjacent to trailhead

> If you're looking for a full-course meal that serves up all the features that make Mineral King great, consider this strenuous hike to Lower Franklin Lake. The approach to the lake traverses verdant Mineral King Valley from north to south, passing through groves of aspen and cottonwoods with stops at cascading waterfalls. From view-packed Farewell Junction, the trail ascends through a colorful amalgam of metamorphic and granitic rock before arriving at the sparkling waters of Franklin Lake.

GETTING THERE

From the junction with North Fork Road and CA Highway 198 in Three Rivers, drive east for 3.8 miles (6.1 km) to Mineral King Road, and turn right. Continue with care on Mineral King Road as it makes its twisting way toward Mineral King Valley

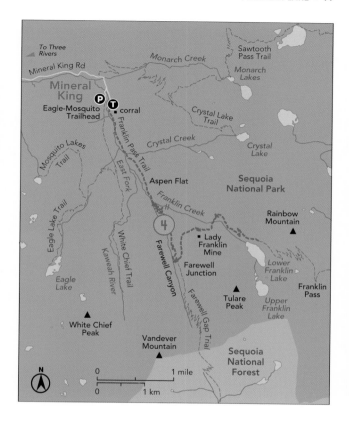

for 24.5 miles (39.4 km), past Atwell Mill Campground and the Mineral King Ranger Station. Turn right onto the access road leading to the Eagle-Mosquito Trailhead, where you will need to park. To reach the Franklin Pass Trailhead, you will have to backtrack to the main road from the Eagle-Mosquito Trailhead, and then turn right onto a dirt access road, which becomes the Franklin Pass Trail. This additional walking adds 0.3 mile (0.5 km) to the total distance.

The impossibly clear waters of Franklin Lake are inviting after a long hike.

ON THE TRAIL

From the information sign indicating the beginning of the Franklin Pass Trail, continue along the dirt road past a gate and then beyond the horse stables at 0.25 mile (0.4 km). Once past the stables, the dirt access road narrows to single-track trail running generally south and parallel to the East Fork Kaweah River. The trail ascends gently through carpets of wildflowers punctuated by occasional groves of black cottonwoods, quaking aspen, red firs, and the occasional solitary Western juniper. The East Fork rumbles along on your right, occasionally meandering close to the trail.

At 1 mile (1.6 km), the trail crosses several branches of Crystal Creek, which cascades several thousand feet down from Crystal Lake to the east. Sharp-eyed hikers may spot an unsigned, abandoned trail leading to Aspen Flat 0.1 mile (0.2 km) beyond Crystal Creek. This is Mineral King's best spot for fall color when the aspens turn gold and red during early October. After the trail's uphill grade increases moderately, the trail crosses Franklin Creek for the first time just below a beautiful multitiered waterfall. Casual hikers who don't want to go all the way to the lake can turn back at the waterfall for a 3.6-mile (5.8-km) roundtrip hike.

Until this point, the amount of uphill work has remained modest, but the climbing can be deferred no longer. Rock-hop over Franklin Creek (a challenging prospect early in the season) and begin a prolonged, mostly exposed series of switchbacks that ascend a grassy ridge dividing Franklin Creek from Farewell Canyon. This first round of switchbacks concludes at 2.6 miles (4.2 km), but the trail maintains a consistent uphill grade as it traverses grassy hillsides above Farewell Canyon heading south. Lofty Vandever Mountain and the V-shaped saddle of Farewell Gap linger ahead, looking more like Scottish highlands than Sierra high country.

Another set of switchbacks culminates at Farewell Junction at 3.7 miles (6 km). This is a great spot for a break with

views north toward Timber Gap and a profusion of wildflowers closer afoot. From Farewell Junction, follow the Franklin
Pass Trail north toward Franklin Creek. After passing through
a spring-laced patch of forest, the trail enters the mouth of
Franklin Creek's hanging valley before ascending to a second crossing of Franklin Creek at 4.6 miles (7.4 km). If you
gaze southeast from this crossing, look for a welcome clue
that your destination is close: a low retaining dam across
Lower Franklin Lake's outlet.

After a handful of switchbacks, the trail approaches and
then climbs above the lake's outlet. Just before the dam at
5.5 miles (8.9 km), look for a side trail on your right leading to potential campsites and the lake's first food storage
locker. The trail continues past these campsites, climbing
125 feet (40 m) above the northern bank of the lake. Once
the trail reaches the route's high point (10,482 feet/3195
m), you reap the rewards of a full view of the Franklin Lakes'
vast basin, with the lakes' translucent waters sparkling in
the High Sierra sun.

At 5.6 miles (9 km) and just beyond a prominent rock outcrop, look for an informal trail that leads toward the banks
of the lower lake and some more possible campsites. This
is the best spot to enjoy the lower lake before making the
long trek back to the trailhead. More camping options and
the lake's second food storage locker lie another 0.2 mile
(0.4 km) along the Franklin Pass Trail.

GOING FARTHER

The Franklin Pass Trail continues climbing from Lower
Franklin Lake until it crests at Franklin Pass. If you want to
punish your quads and calves, continue for another 2 miles
(3.2 km) and 1400 feet (425 m) to reach the pass and stand
high upon the Great Western Divide. Alternatively, you could
tack on a trip to Farewell Gap, which marks Sequoia National

Park's southern boundary with Sequoia National Forest's Golden Trout Wilderness.

5   WHITE CHIEF CANYON

Distance: 7 miles (11.3 km)
Elevation gain: 2200 feet (670 m)
High point: 10,046 feet (3062 m)
Difficulty: Challenging
Trail surface: Dirt
Map: USGS 7.5-min Mineral King
GPS: 36.448477°, -118.595358°
Notes: Suitable for backpacking; food storage lockers near trailhead; restroom near trailhead

As with each of Mineral King's hanging valleys, White Chief Canyon has a character all its own. Spacious meadows and colorful displays of wildflowers contrast with marble outcrops, darker metamorphic rock, lighter granite massifs, and a large glacial cirque laced with meadows and streams. Solitary specimens of Western juniper, Western white pine, and foxtail pine showcase the beautiful forms each species can assume, while carpets of wildflowers brighten the forest floor. A small waterfall greets hikers just below White Chief Bowl, and the views across Mineral King Valley on the approach to White Chief Canyon are superb. Just watch out for mosquitoes, which view White Chief Bowl as prime real estate.

GETTING THERE
From downtown Three Rivers at the junction of North Fork Road and CA Highway 198, head east for 3.8 miles (6.1 km) to Mineral King Road, and turn right. Follow the narrow, twisting road for 24.2 miles (38.9 km) to Mineral King Valley.

Near the end of the road, turn right and cross the East Fork Kaweah River to reach the Eagle-Mosquito Trailhead parking lot.

Meadows and mountain views await on the White Chief Trail.

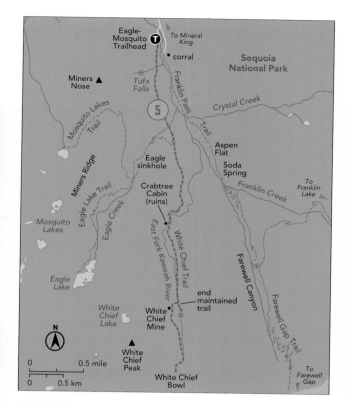

ON THE TRAIL

The trail to White Chief Bowl begins with an oblique ascent along the western slopes of Mineral King Valley on the White Chief Trail. As the trail climbs toward a junction with the Eagle-Mosquito Trail, it passes through occasional forest cover of red fir interspersed with meadows carpeted with sagebrush, ferns, and wildflowers. After the trail crosses a spring-fed creek via a footbridge at 0.25 mile (0.4 km), views begin to open up across Mineral King Valley. The cascading falls of Crystal Creek directly across the valley can be heard as a distant rumble.

Diligent effort leads you to the junction with the Eagle-Mosquito Trail at 1.1 miles (1.8 km). Continue straight past this junction to continue climbing toward White Chief Canyon. The slope's grade increases somewhat, turning the moderate ascent into something decidedly more strenuous. At 1.8 miles (2.9 km), the trail makes a broad arc into the mouth of White Chief Canyon, where picturesque, solitary junipers and pines cling to a harsh existence on rocky metamorphic outcrops. A second switchback straightens the trail out to continue due south as it enters spacious White Chief Canyon. Enjoy a nice break from the climb as the temporarily flat trail traverses a spacious meadow bound on all sides by a colorful mixture of white marble, gray granite, and red-brown metamorphic rock. A spur path at 2 miles (3.2 km) leads to the ruins of Crabtree Cabin.

Continue the traverse through White Chief Canyon to a point where the canyon narrows and the trail approaches a gleaming marble outcrop on the west side of the canyon. At 2.8 miles (4.5 km), look for the shaft for White Chief Mine about 50 feet (15 m) upslope. At this point, the formal trail ends, leaving you with a couple of options. You can scramble up to the mine shaft, but be warned that mines are inherently unstable, and you incur significant risk by entering one. Or you can follow a short spur that continues south to a spot where you get a good look at a 25-foot (8-m) waterfall. Finally, to reach White Chief Bowl, follow the informal path that crosses the creek just below the mine, and continue on the informal path south as it climbs up and over the waterfall and a marble outcrop on the west side of the creek.

After circumventing the waterfall, the trail drops back down to the banks of the creek. At 3.3 miles (5.3 km), the narrow canyon opens up suddenly, revealing a spacious amphitheater rimmed by barren granite. Most basins like this contain a lake, but White Chief Bowl contains a series of meadows and small tarns (tiny mountain lakes) that are quite lovely in their own way. With a little exploration, you will find some good campsites scattered among rocky outcrops looming above these meadows and tarns. Come prepared with good mosquito repellent unless you want to turn into a walking buffet for the resident bloodsuckers.

CRABTREE AND THE WHITE CHIEF

In 1849, prospectors began finding nuggets of gold up and down the length of the Sierra Nevada, leading to a statewide gold boom. By 1872, prospectors began to trickle in to Mineral King, but the avalanche of miners did not start until after James Crabtree filed a claim in a hanging valley riddled with outcrops of gleaming white marble. Crabtree, who was something of a spiritualist, claimed that the ghost of an American Indian appeared to him in a vision and revealed the location of a rich mineral deposit. In tribute to his phantom benefactor, Crabtree named the mine and its environs after the "White Chief," and set about digging into the marble in search of riches.

6 EAGLE LAKE

Distance: 6.8 miles (10.9 km)
Elevation gain: 2400 feet (730 m)
High point: 10,016 feet (3053 m)
Difficulty: Challenging
Trail surface: Dirt
Map: USGS 7.5-min Mineral King
GPS: 36.448477°, -118.595358°
Notes: Suitable for backpacking; food storage locker near trailhead; restroom near trailhead

Eagle Lake is the second of a trio of hanging valleys on the west side of Mineral King Valley that drain into the East Fork Kaweah River. Unlike White Chief Bowl just to the west with its gleaming marble outcrops and dark metamorphic rocks, Eagle Lake and its valley form a picture-perfect image of the classic High Sierra lake basin, complete with lush meadows, talus slopes, abundant evidence of glacial activity, and, of course, a sparkling lake.

GETTING THERE

From downtown Three Rivers at the junction of North Fork Road and CA Highway 198, head east for 3.8 miles (6.1 km) to Mineral King Road, and turn right. Follow the narrow, twisting road for 24.2 miles (38.9 km) to Mineral King Valley. Near the end of the road, turn right and cross the East Fork Kaweah River to reach the Eagle-Mosquito Trailhead parking lot.

ON THE TRAIL

Follow the White Chief Trail south on an oblique climb that traverses Mineral King Valley's western wall. After crossing a spring-fed creek via a footbridge at 0.25 mile (0.4 km), the trail continues to climb through dense groves of red firs alternating with sunny meadows graced with fragrant sagebrush, ferns, and wildflowers. The trail continues on a moderate ascent until the 1.1-mile (1.8-km) mark when it reaches a junction with the Eagle-Mosquito Trail. Turn right here to continue toward Eagle and Mosquito Lakes.

After a sharp switchback leading away from the junction, the trail climbs a sunny hillside meadow rife with summer wildflowers. Switchback your way up this meadow, occasionally pausing to enjoy the developing views north toward Empire Mountain. You earn a respite from the climb as the trail reaches the mouth of Eagle Creek's canyon, where the grade evens out through dense lodgepole forest with a lush understory of grasses and wildflowers. At 1.7 miles (2.7 km),

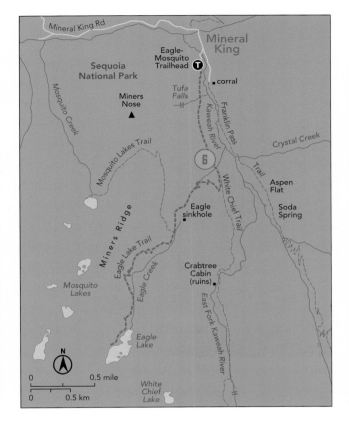

look for a large sinkhole on the east side of the trail. Eagle Creek spills into this sinkhole, from which point it runs underground until it reemerges from a spring just above the sunny meadow you climbed earlier. Continue past the sinkhole as the melodious tones of the creek add a pleasing soundtrack to the shaded stroll through the forest. Continue straight at a junction with the Mosquito Lakes Trail at 1.9 miles (3.1 km).

At 2 miles (3.2 km), the trail resumes its climb away from a marshy meadow and up the western wall of the canyon.

Eagle Lake with views north to Empire Mountain

After working your way over a talus slope, follow a few tight switchbacks before returning to the banks of Eagle Creek once again. The bulk of the climbing is done at this point with only a short, moderate climb remaining to reach Eagle Lake. Be sure to turn back to admire the view toward Empire Mountain and Timber Gap, which become more impressive with every step.

At 3.1 miles (5 km), you reach the northern banks of Eagle Lake. Like several of the other lakes in the Mineral King area, the Mount Whitney Power Company constructed a dam across the lake's inlet. This dam and the ones at Monarch,

Crystal, and Franklin Lakes were a means of controlling the water flow on the East Fork Kaweah River so that the company could harness it for hydroelectric power during the early twentieth century. You can walk across the dam to get a good panoramic view of the lake and its glacial basin. The trail continues along the western banks of Eagle Lake past several camping areas until ending about halfway along the lake.

FOOTHILLS

The four months of peak visitation in the higher elevations (June through September) correspond with the worst possible times to see the foothills, which roast under an unforgiving summer sun. Spring is the best season here because after a winter's worth of rain followed by mild temperatures, the drab, sun-blasted slopes of the five forks of the Kaweah come alive with a riot of vegetation and a dazzling palette of colors from springtime wildflowers. Spring snowmelt at the higher elevations rejuvenates the rivers in a cacophonous spectacle of fury and power, fueling impressive waterfalls. The foothill region's impressive biodiversity showcases a remarkable range of flora and fauna as well as beautiful wildflower displays.

The Foothills area features two campgrounds, Potwisha Campground (open year round; reservations required) and Buckeye Flat Campground (open mid-March to late September; reservations required). Both campgrounds also serve as focal points for recreation along the Middle Fork, with Hospital Rock just west of Buckeye Flat Campground offering picnic tables, restrooms, and a handful of fascinating cultural sites. During the winter, Hospital Rock also doubles as the parking area for the Middle Fork Trailhead, and throughout the year it serves as the parking area for the Paradise Creek Trailhead. The Foothills Visitor Center east of the Ash Mountain Entrance provides information as well as backcountry permits for visitors using the Middle Fork Trail for overnight hikes.

OPPOSITE: *Spring paints the foothills with a colorful palette (Route 9).*

7 POTWISHA PICTOGRAPHS

Distance: 0.8 mile (1.3 km)
Elevation gain: 150 feet (45 m)
High point: 2208 feet (673 m)
Difficulty: Easy
Trail surface: Dirt
Map: USGS 7.5-min Giant Forest
GPS: 36.514922°, -118.800904°
Notes: Day use only; good for kids; restroom at trailhead

This fine introduction to the Foothills area features easy terrain, historic and prehistoric features, and access to a sheltered beach along the Middle Fork Kaweah River that beckons on hot summer days. Although best during March and April, this hike is short and easy, making it safe to hike the route during the scorching summer months, provided you do so very early or very late in the day.

GETTING THERE

From the Ash Mountain Entrance, continue east for 3.8 miles (6.1 km) on Generals Highway to Potwisha Campground. Turn right into the large dirt lot directly across the road from the campground. Keep to the right in order to avoid driving into the RV dump station to the left of the dirt lot. The trailhead lies on the southern end of the lot.

ON THE TRAIL

Head south from the parking area, immediately reaching a sloping granite slab on your right that is riddled with circular depressions. These circular depressions are bedrock mortars (*morteros*), which the indigenous Monache used in conjunction with a pestle to grind out meal from acorns and seeds harvested from the local habitat. About 100 yards

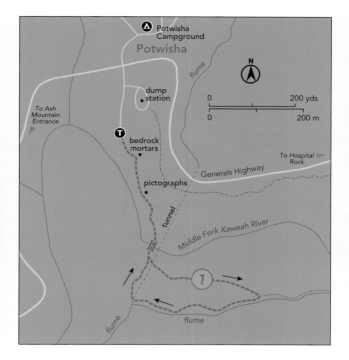

(90 m) south from the slab and about 20 feet (6 m) above the trail, look for a slanting boulder painted over with several pictographs.

Continue past the pictographs through a sandy wash to a suspension bridge crossing the Middle Fork Kaweah River. A small beach in a sheltered cove lies beyond the bridge on the right. The water may look inviting, but use extreme caution since the river's cold temperatures and swift current can be fatal. A large black pipe conveys water from the Marble Fork Flume, which collects water from the Marble Fork Kaweah River just above Potwisha Campground before merging with the flume on the slope above you. Just to the

The old Mount Whitney Power Company flume looks appropriately rustic.

east of the bridge, turn left on a path that passes through a grove of California buckeyes and then climbs toward the Middle Fork's flume.

The two flumes conveyed water downstream to a hydroelectric plant operated by the Mount Whitney Power Company over a century ago. The plant powered communities downstream, providing the first sources of electricity for the burgeoning agricultural communities of Visalia and Tulare. Turn right when you reach the flume to follow a footpath next to the weathered, moss-covered flume through a leafy corridor of oaks.

At 0.6 mile (1 km), you reach a path that descends back toward the footbridge spanning the river. Before descending to the bridge, enjoy the view across Potwisha toward Deep Canyon, through which the Marble Fork Kaweah River runs. Cross the bridge once again and retrace your steps back to the parking area.

8 MARBLE FALLS

Distance: 6.4 miles (10.3 km)
Elevation gain: 1500 feet (460 m)
High point: 3613 feet (1101 m)
Difficulty: Challenging
Trail surface: Dirt
Map: USGS 7.5-min Giant Forest
GPS: 36.518354°, -118.801408°
Notes: Day use only; limited parking; restrooms available within Potwisha Campground

> The Marble Falls Trail traces the course of the Marble Fork Kaweah River en route to a series of cascades that spill over gleaming marble outcrops within the cavernous crease of Deep Canyon. One of the great delights of this trail is experiencing a mosaic of microhabitats shifting between oak woodlands, riparian woodlands, and chaparral that explode with new life and colorful flowers during the heady months of spring.

GETTING THERE

From the Ash Mountain Entrance, drive east for 3.8 miles (6.1 km) on Generals Highway toward Potwisha Campground. Turn left into the campground and bear right at the self-registration kiosk. Make an immediate left on the access road between campsites 32 and 33. The gated dirt road that serves as a trailhead lies to the left of campsite 14 on the north end of the campground.

ON THE TRAIL

The opening segment of this route follows a dirt access road that runs north alongside the Marble Fork Flume. This open flume collects water from the Marble Fork Kaweah River about 0.25 mile (0.4 km) upstream from the hike's start point.

However, you will turn right onto the Marble Falls Trail just before that point at 0.2 mile (0.3 km). The Marble Falls Trail takes one switchback to gain a bit of elevation over the flume access road before settling into a generally northern direction.

As you progress north, the trail darts into and out of shady ravines containing seasonal creeks. Between these ravines, the trail maintains a moderate ascent as it passes through a progression of different habitats that change according to which direction the slope faces. South-facing slopes receive more direct sunshine, thus supporting drought-tolerant plants, such as chamise, ceanothus, and manzanita. North-facing slopes receive less direct sunlight, which allows the soil to maintain more moisture. These slopes support

The Marble Falls Trail at its most verdant

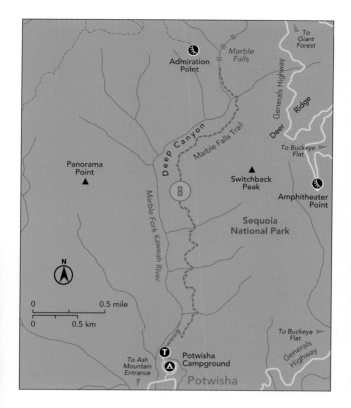

thirstier plants, including live oaks, buckeyes, and fragrant California bay laurels. During April, displays of wildflowers add dashes of color at every step.

After 2.1 miles (3.4 km) of moderate climbing and pleasant passages through the gamut of foothill vegetation, the trail wraps around the base of Switchback Peak to head northeast. From this bend, you can see some of the cascades of the Marble Fork across the canyon. The depths of Deep Canyon add appreciable drama to the scene, and the tree cover becomes permanent as you settle into a final approach to Marble Falls.

The trail comes to an abrupt end at 3.2 miles (5.1 km). Near the end of the trail, the Marble Fork thunders over gleaming outcrops of marble in an impressive cascade. Several other cascades lie upstream, and when the water level isn't too high, you may be able to pick your way over boulders with great caution for a short distance. Watch out for poison oak, and definitely don't go any farther than the end of the trail if the water is high. Otherwise, you invite disaster from the swift-moving river.

9   PARADISE CREEK

Distance: 5.6 miles (9 km)
Elevation gain: 1600 feet (490 m)
High point: 3851 feet (1174 m)
Difficulty: Challenging
Trail surface: Dirt
Map: USGS 7.5-min Giant Forest
GPS: 36.520973°, -118.771355°
Notes: Day use only; restrooms available at Hospital Rock and within Buckeye Flat Campground

Undeniably lovely, Paradise Creek lives up to its name. The creek's waters, born in the highlands of Paradise Ridge, nurture a lush mixture of oak and buckeye woodlands, riparian woodlands, and a low-elevation coniferous forest that persists thanks to abundant moisture and deep shade. Several smaller cascades and two medium-sized waterfalls will delight hikers who enjoy the effects of gravity on water. The off-the-beaten path location of the route provides a healthy dose of solitude for a peaceful and verdant hiking experience.

GETTING THERE

From the Ash Mountain Entrance, drive east on Generals Highway for 6 miles (9.7 km) to the Hospital Rock parking lot, trailhead, and picnic area. There is no day-use parking for the Paradise Creek Trailhead within Buckeye Flat Campground, and hikers will need to park at Hospital Rock and walk along the 0.6-mile (1-km) Buckeye Flat Campground access road leading to the campground to reach the trailhead. The Paradise Creek Trailhead lies directly across from campsite 28 within Buckeye Flat Campground.

ON THE TRAIL

Before you start the hike, or perhaps on the return trip, consider a quick diversion down a paved path that descends from the east side of Generals Highway to the banks of

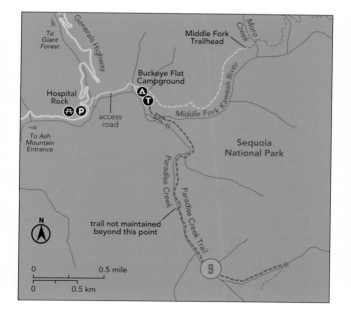

The Middle Fork Kaweah River roars past green hillsides in spring.

the Middle Fork Kaweah River. Impressive cascades, a cave, and a viewpoint make this a pleasant spot to explore. A large slab of bedrock mortars sits directly across the road from Hospital Rock, a well-preserved panel of pictographs so named because the indigenous Monache attended to the wounds of an early European American explorer near this spot.

The initial stretch of road walking from Hospital Rock to Buckeye Flat passes through a pleasant assortment of grassy hillsides, oak woodlands, and occasional riparian gallery forests of sycamores. After 0.6 mile (1 km), turn right onto the road leading into Buckeye Flat Campground. Keep left and look for the Paradise Creek Trailhead adjacent to campsite 28. The Paradise Creek Trail follows the banks of the Middle Fork beneath a dense canopy of buckeyes before reaching a bridge spanning the river. During March and April, the usually dry slopes above the river come alive in a palette of greens splashed with vivid orange from fields of California poppies. Depending on the state of the snowpack, the Middle Fork may be swollen, with its heavy flow crashing and careening through the bottom of the canyon.

After crossing the river, the trail enters the mouth of Paradise Creek's canyon. Just before winding through a grove of ponderosa pines and incense cedars, the trail passes above a small bowl gouged out of red metamorphic rock. Paradise Creek spills into this bowl, creating a small but beautiful waterfall. On warm days, the pool beneath the falls may prove a temptation too great to resist. Children may enjoy hiking this far, but the trail becomes steeper and rougher ahead, creating a challenge for smaller children.

Beyond the falls, the trail passes through a pine grove before bending to the south to parallel Paradise Creek about 20 to 100 feet upslope (5 to 30 m). As you progress, be sure to look back from time to time to catch glimpses of Moro Rock protruding from the Giant Forest plateau over 3000 feet (915 m) above to the north. Water-loving white alders and occasional conifers crowd along the creek, which spills over numerous small cascades. Upslope, scattered oaks and buckeyes stand upon grassy hillsides splashed with orange, yellow, and blue from seasonal wildflowers.

The maintained trail ends at a creek crossing at the 1.8-mile (2.9-km) mark. From here, the unmaintained path becomes progressively rougher, although it is not difficult to keep to the path. The bigger issue is encroaching vegetation and uneven terrain. Perform regular tick checks to make sure no hitchhikers sink their mandibles in for unmitigated blood-sucking. The trail doubles back across the creek at 1.9 miles (3.1 km) and begins to arc to the east. At 2.4 miles (3.9 km), the trail splits away from Paradise Creek to follow an often-dry tributary.

The route ends at a second waterfall (2.8 miles/4.5 km) that is more secluded but not as beautiful as the one earlier on. Although the Paradise Creek Trail historically continued beyond this waterfall along the Castle Rocks ridge up to the crest of Paradise Ridge, the route is now almost entirely lost due to encroaching chaparral. Although you can continue for a short distance beyond the waterfall, there isn't much to see. Therefore, the second waterfall is your turnaround point.

10   MIDDLE FORK TRAIL TO PANTHER CREEK

Distance: 6.1 miles (9.8 km)
Elevation gain: 1200 feet (370 m)
High point: 3975 feet (1212 m)
Difficulty: Challenging
Trail surface: Dirt
Map: USGS 7.5-min Giant Forest
GPS: 36.527535°, -118.751373°
Notes: Suitable for backpacking; no restroom at trailhead, but restrooms are available at Hospital Rock

> Nearly all of the watercourses west of the Great Western Divide in Sequoia National Park drain a vast landscape ranging from foothills at 1000 feet (305 m) of elevation all the way up to snowcapped alpine peaks crowning the divide. In the center of this watershed runs the Middle Fork Kaweah River's canyon, a deep V-shaped gash in the earth that features some of the most spectacular scenery in the park. The Middle Fork Trail follows the course of this river through a kaleidoscope of foothill habitats set against peaks towering 3000–8000 feet (915–2440 m) above the canyon floor.

GETTING THERE

From the Ash Mountain Entrance, drive east on Generals Highway for 6 miles (9.7 km) to the Hospital Rock parking lot, trailhead, and picnic area. If the road to Buckeye Flat is open, follow the road 0.5 mile (0.7 km) to the junction with the campground. Turn left onto the dirt road leading to the Middle Fork Trail another 0.7 mile (1.1 km) beyond. The road to Buckeye Flat Campground is closed from October

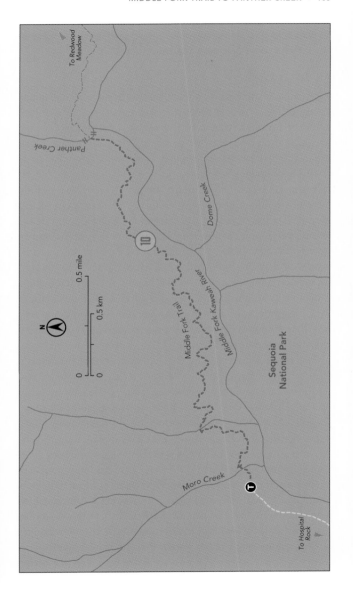

to March. If you're visiting during that time, park at Hospital Rock Picnic Area and walk the road to the trailhead.

ON THE TRAIL

From the Middle Fork Trailhead, make a quick descent to the banks of Moro Creek. Moro Creek drains the southern half of Giant Forest, and its contents spill over a pretty waterfall just above an unimproved crossing. From the Moro Creek crossing, the trail heads generally east, weaving in and out of a variety of ravines, some of which contain water. Each angle of the slope—west, east, south, and north—reveals a slightly different floral arrangement. South- and southwest-facing slopes feature chaparral dominated by chamise and cean-othus and punctuated by tree-sized specimens of manzanita and the showy blossoms of flannel bush. East- and south-east-facing slopes feature mostly live oaks and California bay. Grassy sections between the two plant communities feature a profusion of wildflowers, including annuals like owl's clover and poppy. Yuccas, a once-in-a-lifetime flowering plant with sharp, needlelike leaves, shoot up stalks crowned with large, cream-colored flower clusters.

The views encompassing the higher points of the Middle Fork's canyon begin to take on greater prominence as you progress. Many of the visible formations, including Castle Rocks, Paradise Peak, Moro Rock, and the Great Western Divide, appear formidable and grand from this lower van-tage. Snow often coats the higher elevations through win-ter and spring, and the Great Western Divide lies beneath a heavy snowpack well into spring and early summer.

The vegetation begins a transition upon approaching Pan-ther Creek. Live oaks and bays give way to a smattering of conifers and a few deciduous black oaks, golden-leaved in fall. This shift in flora heralds the transition from woodlands and chaparral into proper forest. Panther Creek offers good camping (no food storage) and access to the creek just below

The soaring, snow-covered peaks of the Great Western Divide

a pretty waterfall and a deep pool that invites summertime swimming. An even more impressive waterfall tumbles over a cliff into the Middle Fork just below, but dangerous cliffs will prevent you from getting a good look. Note that Panther Creek can become impassable during periods of heavy snowmelt, usually between March and May. If so, it's unwise to continue any farther than the creek.

GOING FARTHER

The Middle Fork Trail penetrates deep into the Middle Fork's canyon until terminating at Redwood Meadow, 11.4 miles (18.3 km) from the Middle Fork Trailhead. Day hikers starting from the Middle Fork Trailhead can hike to Mehrten Creek (a 12-mile/19-km roundtrip hike), which boasts a 20-foot (6-m) waterfall and dramatic views of the Great Western Divide. Backpackers can continue all the way to Redwood Meadow, or they can turn north to climb up to Bearpaw Meadow's High Sierra Camp for a three-day, 25.6-mile (41.2-km) out-and-back excursion.

GIANT FOREST

Within the confines of Giant Forest, hikers will encounter some of the largest trees on the planet in a sequoia grove so abundantly rich that its "average" trees would be the monarchs of other groves. Several emerald meadows containing a riot of greenery dot the forest, setting the stage for the antics of wildlife as well as providing perspectives from which to consider 250-foot (75-m) Goliaths. A collection of granite outcrops offers ideal sunset-viewing spots and vistas toward the towering ramparts of the Great Western Divide and the depths of the Middle Fork Canyon thousands of feet below. A superb network of trails provides on-foot access to a spectrum of experiences ranging from short, kid-friendly hikes featuring meadows and rock outcrops to half-day hikes deep into the grove.

Trailheads providing access to the Giant Forest trail network can be found at four main hubs of activity: the Giant Forest Museum located on the southwest corner of the grove; the Moro Rock Trailhead on the southern margin of the grove; Crescent Meadow on the southeast corner of the grove; and the General Sherman Trailhead and parking area on the northern margins of the grove. Interconnectivity between these four main hubs coupled with an easy-to-navigate shuttle system running from mid-May to late September creates the potential for a lot of extended exploration beyond the routes presented here. Each description in this chapter indicates which shuttle you can take to the trailhead.

OPPOSITE: *Shooting stars and sequoias at Circle Meadow (Route 17)*

A few special cautions apply to hiking in Giant Forest. Visitors must keep in mind that the grove supports a very large and active bear population. While the bears will show little interest in you, their presence makes following food storage rules imperative. Additionally, you must always stay out of the meadows; your heavy footsteps can damage meadow habitats, which take a long time to recover. Do your best to remain on-trail. Not only is it easy to get lost, but much of the forest is still recovering from decades of heavy use; staying on the trails helps to facilitate that recovery. Additionally, dispersed camping is forbidden within Giant Forest and nearby areas to prevent further overuse.

The Giant Forest trail network also caters to winter activities such as snowshoeing and cross-country skiing. Several of the trails double as winter routes, and the park marks these routes using yellow triangles emblazoned with a symbol denoting a specific trail. Each of the descriptions within this chapter provides information on winter routes where appropriate, but if you plan to visit the forest during winter, it is best to purchase a winter trail map from the visitor center and museum. Note that Crescent Meadow Road closes during the winter, and when it's covered in snow, it makes a good snowshoeing route between the museum and Crescent Meadow.

11 BEETLE ROCK

Distance: 1.1 miles (1.8 km)
Elevation gain: 150 feet (45 m)
High point: 6455 feet (1967 m)
Difficulty: Easy
Trail surface: Dirt
Map: USGS 7.5-min Giant Forest
GPS: 36.564723°, -118.773375°
Notes: Day use only; good for kids; restroom at the trailhead

Beetle Rock is the first of four distinct granite outcrops offering fantastic sunset views from the edge of the Giant Forest plateau. Like the other outcrops, Beetle Rock's views as well as its opportunities for pleasant, casual exploration attract a variety of visitors, especially families. Children and less experienced hikers will also have an easy time with the gentle topography and rich array of sights packed into a short loop. Even experienced hikers may enjoy this route as a sunset digestif to cap off a day of exploring Giant Forest.

Beetle Rock offers great sunset viewing.

GETTING THERE

Driving: From the Ash Mountain Entrance, head north on Generals Highway for 16.4 miles (26.4 km) to the parking area for the Giant Forest Museum on the left side of the road.

Transit: Green Route 1 runs from Giant Forest Museum to Lodgepole. Gray Route 2 runs from Giant Forest Museum to Crescent Meadow. The Visalia Route (Blue) runs from Visalia to Giant Forest Museum (fee and reservations required).

ON THE TRAIL

Despite the rock's vague resemblance to a beetle, this destination's moniker actually stems from an entomologist's discovery of a rare beetle while exploring the outcrop. The nearby Beetle Rock Family Nature Center reflects this tradition of scientific discovery. The nature center is open from June through August between 10:00 AM and 4:00 PM.

To begin, turn left at the bottom of the staircase leading to the crosswalk over Generals Highway. Follow the paved path along the road and curve to the left to reach a dirt path signed for Sunset Rock that turns north and skirts the edge of a small meadow. Black bears enjoy frolicking in this meadow, and their antics often cause evening traffic jams on Generals Highway as spectators attempt to watch the animals from the road. This short section of trail offers a more intimate and less hectic vantage from which to view bears, which may or may not actually make you feel more comfortable.

After crossing Little Deer Creek by footbridge at 0.2 mile (0.3 km), take a left to follow a west-trending trail instead of continuing north toward Sunset Rock. The trail crosses Little Deer Creek again shortly after the bridge before wrapping around a hillside on a wide arc to the south. As you progress along the south-facing slope, deciduous black oaks (golden in October and early November) join Jeffrey pines and incense cedars on the drier, sunnier terrain.

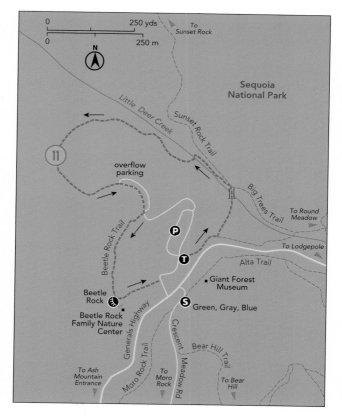

One slight navigational obstacle occurs when you reach the edge of an overflow parking lot at 0.75 mile (1.2 km). Keep to the right side of the parking lot as it curves toward a restroom and the inlet road, and keep right to find the path leading to Beetle Rock at the 1-mile (1.6-km) mark. Once you reach the outcrop, travel is free-form over the exposed granite surface. Sunset viewing can be outstanding, and there are numerous opportunities for children to poke into various nooks and crannies. When finished, a short paved route past the nature center leads you back to the parking lot.

GOING FARTHER

You can combine the Beetle Rock route with either or both the Sunset Rock (Route 12) and Round Meadow (Route 13) routes for a more extensive but still gentle exploration of the Giant Forest Museum area.

12 SUNSET ROCK

Distance: 1.8 miles (2.9 km)
Elevation gain: 200 feet (60 m)
High point: 6455 feet (1967 m)
Difficulty: Easy
Trail surface: Dirt
Map: USGS 7.5-min Giant Forest
GPS: 36.564723°, -118.773375°
Notes: Day use only; good for kids; restroom adjacent to trailhead; snowshoeing route

Sunset Rock is one of several different granitic outcrops with superb views to the west. As its moniker would suggest, the rock makes a fine spot for viewing sunsets, even if Colony Peak to the west sometimes obscures the actual sunset moment during the late-spring and summer months. A short trip along a pocket meadow followed by gentle forest rambling round out this peaceful experience.

GETTING THERE

Driving: From the Ash Mountain Entrance, head north on Generals Highway for 16.4 miles (26.4 km) to the parking area for the Giant Forest Museum on the left side of the road.

Transit: Green Route 1 runs from Giant Forest Museum to Lodgepole. Gray Route 2 runs from Giant Forest Museum to Crescent Meadow. The Visalia Route (Blue) runs from Visalia to Giant Forest Museum (fee and reservations required).

ON THE TRAIL

From the Giant Forest Museum parking area, descend the covered staircase and turn left onto the paved trail before

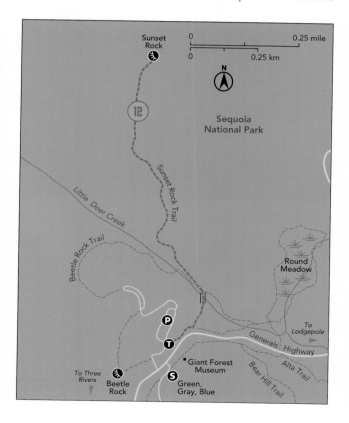

Yellow-throated gilia carpets the Sunset Rock Trail.

reaching the crosswalk that leads to the museum. After 0.1 mile (0.2 km), turn left onto a dirt path signed for Sunset Rock that skirts the edge of a small meadow. Cross a wooden bridge over Little Deer Creek and continue straight at the signed junction for the Sunset Rock Trail on the north side of the bridge. This trail is one of several in Giant Forest marked for snowshoeing; the yellow triangles nailed to trees along the route guide snowshoers when the trail is obscured by snow.

Follow the trail north, first through sequoia forest and then later through open groves of black oaks, Jeffrey pine, and manzanita. After 0.6 mile (1 km), the trail reaches a clearing, where the large, polished outcrop of Sunset Rock affords fine views west across the deep folds of the Marble Fork Kaweah River's rugged canyon and beyond to the foothills. Numerous flat areas atop Sunset Rock invite picnicking and repose, making it an excellent place to enjoy the sinking sun. While the trail back to the museum is easy enough to follow in the post-sunset gloaming, bring a headlamp to make sure you don't lose your way.

GOING FARTHER

You can combine the trail to Sunset Rock with either or both the Beetle Rock (Route 11) and Round Meadow (Route 13) routes for a more extensive but still gentle exploration of the Giant Forest Museum area.

13   ROUND MEADOW

Distance: 1.3 miles (2.1 km)
Elevation gain: 100 feet (30 m)
High point: 6455 feet (1967 m)
Difficulty: Easy
Trail surface: Paved, dirt, and boardwalk around the meadow
Map: USGS 7.5-min Giant Forest
GPS: 36.564723°, -118.773375°
Notes: Day use only; good for kids; toilets at trailhead; accessible trail; snowshoeing route

This fine introduction to the Giant Forest area samples sequoia forest with a few notable trees, a pristine meadow, and an easy trail suitable for everybody. Although this area was once a bustling hub of activity, including gas stations, restaurants, tent cabins, campgrounds, and a store, the park's long-term restoration of it has produced a rejuvenated habitat showcasing Giant Forest at its best.

GETTING THERE

Driving: From the Ash Mountain Entrance, head north on Generals Highway for 16.4 miles (26.4 km) to the parking area for the Giant Forest Museum on the left side of the road.

Transit: Green Route 1 runs from Giant Forest Museum to Lodgepole. Gray Route 2 runs from Giant Forest Museum to Crescent Meadow. The Visalia Route (Blue) runs from Visalia to Giant Forest Museum (fee and reservations required).

ON THE TRAIL

Before you set out on this hike, consider taking a quick stop at the Giant Forest Museum. To find the museum, walk from the parking area down a flight of stairs that leads to a crosswalk spanning Generals Highway. The museum lies on the opposite side of the road, and inside you will find interpretive displays and helpful rangers to provide all of the support you'll need.

If you opt to skip the museum, descend the stairs from the parking area and, before reaching the crosswalk, turn left onto the paved path. Continue along the sidewalk next to Generals Highway, passing the start of the Sunset Rock Trail

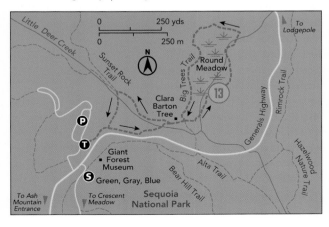

Twin sequoias stand sentinel at Round Meadow.

and heading east along the edge of a small meadow before the trail veers away from the road and across Little Deer Creek at 0.25 mile (0.4 km). Shortly beyond this crossing, the trail reaches the beginning of the Big Trees Trail at its starting point from the accessible parking area.

Once you reach the Big Trees Trail, head counterclockwise around the oval meadow on alternating pavement and boardwalk. Interpretive signs along the way detail meadow ecology, and the paved outline of a fallen giant on the southwest side of the meadow gives perspective on just how massive the bases of sequoia trees can be. The meadow bursts forth with a bewildering array of wildflowers, butterflies, and wildlife throughout the summer while providing a clear, circular snowshoeing route during winter.

Upon reaching the southwest corner of the meadow and returning to the accessible parking area, find a path leading away from the lot that parallels the north side of Generals

Highway. You'll pass the Clara Barton Tree, one of only a few trees in the grove named after a woman, before passing through a small meadow frequented by black bears. At 1.1 miles (1.8 km), turn left at the junction for Sunset Rock and an unsigned trail leading to Beetle Rock. Cross the bridge over Little Deer Creek, and continue south to the highway. Turn right to follow the paved trail back to the parking area.

GOING FARTHER

You can combine the route to Round Meadow with either or both the Beetle Rock (Route 11) and Sunset Rock (Route 12) routes for a more extensive but still gentle exploration of the Giant Forest Museum area.

14 SOLDIERS LOOP

Distance: 4.2 miles (6.8 km)
Elevation gain: 800 feet (240 m)
High point: 6824 feet (2080 m)
Difficulty: Moderate
Trail surface: Dirt
Map: USGS 7.5-min Giant Forest
GPS: 36.564723°, -118.773375°
Notes: Day use only; restrooms adjacent to trailhead

This lightly traveled route takes you deep into a seldom-visited corner of Giant Forest by way of an old trail created by the buffalo soldiers who first protected the park. Hanging Rock, a precipitously balanced slab of granite, offers a midway stopping point with phenomenal sunset views that also take in Moro Rock and the Castle Rocks. Early spring brings a proliferation of dogwood blooms at various points along both the Soldiers Trail as well as the Moro Rock Trail that completes the loop.

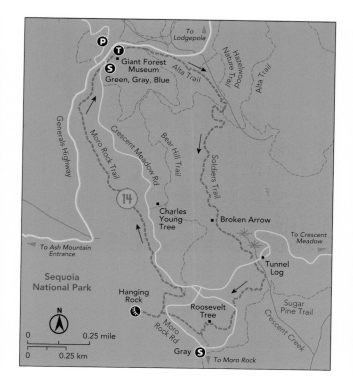

GETTING THERE

Driving: From the Ash Mountain Entrance, head north on Generals Highway for 16.4 miles (26.4 km) to the parking area for the Giant Forest Museum on the left side of the road. To reach the trailhead, cross Generals Highway and turn left at the museum. You will find the Alta Trailhead a short distance east from the museum.

Transit: Green Route 1 runs from Giant Forest Museum to Lodgepole. Gray Route 2 runs from Giant Forest Museum to Crescent Meadow. The Visalia Route (Blue) runs from Visalia to Giant Forest Museum (fee and reservations required).

Hanging Rock enjoys a sunset from its precarious perch.

ON THE TRAIL

From the trailhead, head east on the Alta Trail, initially paralleling Generals Highway before bending right into a lush ravine containing a narrow meadow fed by a tributary of Little Deer Creek. Beautiful thickets of mountain dogwood crowd in along the trail. During late May, the dogwoods burst forth with showy white blossoms. Continue straight past junctions for the Bear Hill Trail on the right, the Hazelwood Nature Trail on the left, and another leg of the Bear Hill Trail on the right. At 0.7 mile (1.1 km), veer right onto the signed Soldiers Trail as it peels away from the Alta Trail.

Once on the Soldiers Trail, commence a steep climb out of Little Deer Creek's ravine up and over a ridge. After huffing and puffing your way up the 400-foot (120-m) ascent, the trail tops out and then commences a gentle descent through spacious sequoia forest. Not long after the ridge, look for a blackened sequoia stump that resembles a broken arrow shaft plunged into the ground named, fittingly, Broken Arrow. At 1.4 miles (2.3 km), the trail reaches another lush meadow. The soldiers who once guarded Giant Forest during the park's inception kept their barracks here, and they blazed the original Soldiers Trail as a shortcut to the Giant Forest Museum area.

Cross Crescent Meadow Road west of Tunnel Log (a short walk away, if you want to explore it) and follow the continuation of the trail south above a branch of Crescent Creek. After passing into and out of a shallow ravine, the Soldiers Trail crosses Moro Rock Road and climbs to the Roosevelt Tree before dropping back down toward the Moro Rock parking area. Just before the Moro Rock parking area, turn right onto a spur trail that parallels the road. If you want to tack on Moro Rock (Route 15), cut south across the parking area to find the beginning of the granite staircase that climbs to the summit.

COLONEL YOUNG AND THE BUFFALO SOLDIERS

From the inception of Sequoia National Park, park rangers had no directive and overriding philosophy toward preservation, which resulted in piecemeal efforts to protect Giant Forest and establish infrastructure that could enable visitation. A group of black soldiers from the 9th US Cavalry, known as buffalo soldiers, led by Colonel Charles Young, the third African American graduate from West Point, began patrolling the forest to protect it from private economic interests. Young later became the park's first superintendent, and during his tenure, he completed an impressive amount of improvements, including the completion of the first road into Giant Forest. Young has a tree named after him, which lies just to the west of the Bear Hill Trail.

The trail crosses Moro Rock Road for a second time to reach the short spur trail leading to Hanging Rock. Hanging Rock, an angular granite slab, perches atop the rim of the Giant Forest plateau, and the views into Middle Fork Kaweah Canyon will not fail to impress. Hikers may observe outstanding sunsets from this point, although that usually means a walk back in dusky gloom to the museum.

Retrace your steps back to Moro Rock Road and turn left onto the Moro Rock Trail that leads north to the Giant Forest Museum. The trail parallels Crescent Meadow Road, but traffic noise is rarely apparent. Before reaching the museum, you'll pass through an old burn zone where breaks in the trees offer a few slivers of view toward Colony Peak and the Ash Peaks Ridge. The trail comes to an end at Crescent Meadow Road just a few dozen yards west of the shuttle stops for the Giant Forest Museum.

GOING FARTHER

As mentioned in the trip description, you can tack on an optional trip up to Moro Rock (Route 15) for an additional 0.5 mile (0.8 km) and 300 feet (90 m) of elevation gain.

15   MORO ROCK

Distance: 0.5 mile (0.8 km)
Elevation gain: 300 feet (90 m)
High point: 6725 feet (2050 m)
Difficulty: Moderate
Trail surface: Granite
Map: USGS 7.5-min Giant Forest
GPS: 36.546909°, -118.765612°
Notes: Day use only; good for older kids; restroom at trailhead

Sunrise illuminates a spring inversion layer above Middle Fork Canyon.

The marvelously engineered route to the top of Moro Rock is less of a hike and more of a vertiginous Stairmaster session. The short, steep climb reaches the top of Sequoia's signature exfoliation dome. From the summit, a magnificent panorama spreads from the towering pinnacles of the Great Western Divide down to the distant waters of Lake Kaweah—an elevation spread of over 12,000 feet (3660 km)!

GETTING THERE

Driving: From the Ash Mountain Entrance, drive north for 16.4 miles (26.4 km) along winding Generals Highway, and turn right onto Crescent Meadow Road. Continue for 1.2 miles (1.9 km) to a junction with Moro Rock Road and make a slight right. Keep right on the one-way loop road, and after 0.4 mile (0.6), arrive at the Moro Rock parking area.

Transit: Gray Route 2 stops at Moro Rock. Note that during peak times (mid-May to mid-September), the park may close Crescent Meadow Road to automobile traffic, at which time the shuttle is the only way to reach Moro Rock Trailhead without a long hike from the Giant Forest Museum.

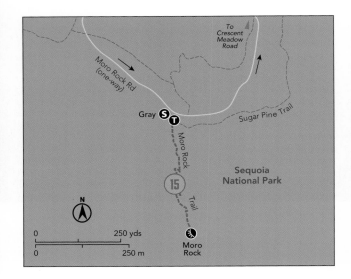

ON THE TRAIL

From the parking area, pass a series of interpretive panels describing the geology of Moro Rock and the history of the staircase. Keep right to locate the steep staircase, and begin climbing along the east side of Moro Rock's spine. Completed in 1931, the Moro Rock staircase replaced an older wooden staircase that climbed straight along the spine of the dome. The trail's inconspicuous nature, superb engineering, and historic character led to its addition to the National Register of Historic Places.

Moro Rock itself is an exfoliation dome. *Exfoliation* refers to the granitic rock's tendency to slough off in layers, while the term *dome* describes the shape. Such domes are common in the Sierra Nevada, most notably in Yosemite National Park. This dome began its existence as a subterranean pool of magma that slowly rose to the surface, cooling gradually. Overlying rock eroded away over time, revealing the large rounded granite mass. Exfoliation has continued ever since, with frost wedging—a process where water freezes in cracks, pushing layers of rock apart—being the driving force in ongoing erosion.

Three hundred fifty breathless steps lead you to the summit, from which point you will enjoy a magnificent panorama encompassing the entirety of the Middle Fork Kaweah Canyon, the Giant Forest plateau, and the Great Western Divide. Sunsets from the summit are among the best in the parks. Hikers should avoid attempting to climb Moro Rock in snowy or icy conditions, as a fall from the steep staircase could be fatal. Similarly, hikers should also avoid the summit during thunderstorms, as lightning strikes are common.

16 SUGAR PINE TRAIL

Distance: 3 miles (4.8 km)
Elevation gain: 700 feet (210 m)
High point: 6795 feet (2017 m)
Difficulty: Moderate
Trail surface: Dirt
Map: USGS 7.5-min Giant Forest
GPS: 36.546939°, -118.765263°
Notes: Day use only; good for kids; restroom at the trailhead and farther along at Crescent Meadow

This lightly traveled lollipop loop features the other giant of Giant Forest: the sugar pine. This species attains the greatest heights of the pine species, and its graceful spreading boughs dangle massive pinecones as if mischievously waiting to plunk unsuspecting hikers below. Soaring views from Bobcat Point and a stop at Crescent Meadow add variety to the route. A small pond along Crescent Creek is one of the hidden beauty spots of Giant Forest.

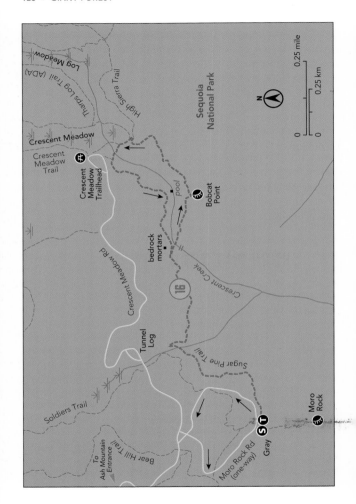

GETTING THERE

Driving: From the Ash Mountain Entrance, drive north for 16.4 miles (26.4 km) along winding Generals Highway, and turn right onto Crescent Meadow Road. Continue for 1.2

miles (1.9 km) to a junction with Moro Rock road and make a slight right. Keep right on the one-way loop road, and after 0.4 mile (0.6 km), arrive at the Moro Rock parking area.

Transit: Gray Route 2 stops at Moro Rock. Note that during peak times (mid-May to mid-September), the park may close Crescent Meadow Road to automobile traffic, at which time the shuttle is the only way to reach the Sugar Pine Trail without a long hike from the Giant Forest Museum.

ON THE TRAIL

You will find the unassuming but signed trailhead for the Sugar Pine Trail to the left of the Moro Rock staircase. The Sugar Pine Trail descends gently from the bustling Moro Rock Trailhead along the southern rim of the Giant Forest plateau. Given the south-facing slope aspect, the vegetation on the Sugar Pine Trail is drier than the rest of Giant Forest. Drier conditions lead to more drought-tolerant tree species, like Jeffrey pines and black oaks, although some sequoias can be found in a handful of drainages and by Crescent Meadow in the middle of the loop.

After passing in and out of a pair of ravines, the trail passes through mixed-conifer forest dominated by sugar pines. This massive pine reaches heights of 270 feet (80 m), and its pinecones grow up to 1.5 feet (0.3 m) long, making it both the largest pine species on the planet and producer of the largest of all the pinecones. This conifer owes its name to its sweet sap, which American Indians used as a sweetener. To identify the tree, look for the foot-long pinecones littering the base as well as the slender branches radiating from the trunk as telltale identifiers.

At 0.9 mile (1.4 km), the trail splits. Just before the split, you will hear the sound of Crescent Creek spilling over a rocky outcrop to your right. Follow a short spur path that leads to a spot where you can view a small waterfall. Just beyond this junction, a second spur trail leads to a set

The Castle Rocks and Paradise Ridge viewed from Bobcat Point

of bedrock mortars used by the local indigenous people during summer periods when they kept a migratory camp atop Giant Forest. Keep right and cross Crescent Creek to begin a steep climb along a ridge to Bobcat Point. This vista point features a sweeping panorama that ranges from Moro Rock to the Great Western Divide. From Bobcat Point, the trail continues to climb, albeit more gently, until it crests a ridge and drops down to a junction with the High Sierra Trail.

At the High Sierra Trail junction, turn left to connect to the paved Crescent Meadow Trail. Once at the Crescent Meadow Trail, turn left again to begin the return journey from the southern tip of the meadow. Keep left on an unsigned trail just before a footbridge spanning Crescent Creek. This connecting trail crosses Crescent Creek and continues to descend gently along the creek until arriving at a beautiful pool at 1.9 miles (3.1 km). Insects skim across the surface of the pool, which is surrounded by a riot of lush riparian vegetation beneath the towering pillars of sequoias, firs, and pines.

Just beyond the pool, the trail reconnects with the Sugar Pine Trail, closing the loop. Retrace your steps west back to Moro Rock.

GOING FARTHER

When you reach the junction with the Crescent Meadow Trail, you have the option of either tacking on the short loop around Crescent Meadow or adding the full Crescent and Log Meadows loop (Route 18).

17 CIRCLE MEADOW

Distance: 4 miles (6.4 km)
Elevation gain: 650 feet (200 m)
High point: 7118 feet (2170 m)
Difficulty: Moderate
Trail surface: Dirt
Map: USGS 7.5-min Giant Forest
GPS: 36.554855°, -118.749003°
Notes: Day use only; good for kids; restroom at the trailhead; winter snowshoeing route

Where the marshy headwaters of Little Deer Creek hug the base of a gentle knoll, the sluggish flow of water creates a narrow C-shaped meadow that comes alive—in season—with a colorful palette of wildflowers. This lollipop loop wraps around Circle Meadow while also stopping at some of the largest sequoias in Giant Forest and the historic Cattle Cabin site.

GETTING THERE

Driving: From the Ash Mountain Entrance, drive north for 16.4 miles (26.4 km) along winding Generals Highway, and turn right onto Crescent Meadow Road. Continue for 1.2 miles (1.9 km) to a junction with Moro Rock Road and make a slight left to stay on Crescent Meadow Road. After another 1.3 miles (2.1 km), the road terminates at the Crescent Meadow/High Sierra Trailhead.

Transit: Gray Route 2 stops at Crescent Meadow. Note that the park may close Crescent Meadow Road to automobile traffic during the peak season (mid-May to mid-September),

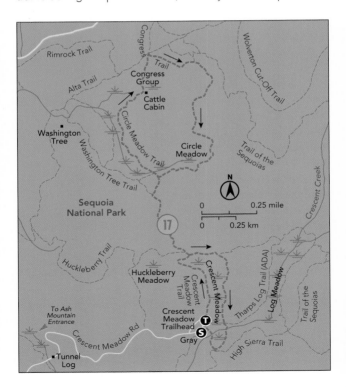

Snowshoeing the Circle Meadow Trail

during which time the shuttle is the only way to access the trailhead.

ON THE TRAIL

From the Crescent Meadow Trailhead, look for a trail on the northeast corner of the parking area that heads north along the west edge of Crescent Meadow. Follow this trail north for 0.4 mile (0.6 km) along the meadow to a pair of junctions in close succession. The first junction accesses trails that head east to Log Meadow and south along the east edge of Crescent Meadow. Keep left at this junction. The second junction accesses a trail leading west toward Huckleberry Meadow. Huckleberry Meadow is a worthwhile side trip if you have the time; the out-and-back diversion will add 0.5 mile (0.8 km) of hiking to your roundtrip total. To follow the remainder of the route, keep right at the Huckleberry Meadow junction to continue heading north toward Circle Meadow.

After the junctions, follow the trail north as it climbs up and over a densely wooded saddle to reach a second set of junctions at 0.8 mile (1.3 km). Keep right at the first junction, where a trail leads west toward the Washington Tree. Shortly after this junction, you reach a second junction with the loop trail that encircles Circle Meadow. Keep left here to cross the meadow and continue north along its eastern edge. As you progress, keep your eyes peeled for a host of wildlife browsing for food in the long, narrow strip of lush vegetation on your left. Black bears, deer, marmots, and an armada of birds haunt this meadow, particularly in the early morning and evening.

At 1.4 miles (2.3 km), the trail reaches Cattle Cabin, a wooden structure left over from the early days of the park. Park butchers used to graze cattle in the nearby meadow, and they would slaughter the cows to provide beef for visitors. Today, the cabin looks appropriately rustic, but all traces of bovines have long since vanished. Continue north for another 0.2 mile (0.3 km) and arrive at a five-way junction with the Alta Trail and the Congress Trail. After taking a moment to review the map on a kiosk placed next to the junction, turn right on the Congress Trail and continue for another 0.2 mile (0.3 km) to a continuation of the Circle Meadow Trail. Keep right at this junction as you begin the return journey back to Crescent Meadow.

The trail climbs over the ridge that separates the two arms of Circle Meadow before returning back to the earlier junction with the Washington Tree Trail and the trail back to Crescent Meadow. Keep left at these two successive junctions at 2.7 miles (4.3 km) and 2.8 miles (4.5 km). This will place you southbound on the trail back to Crescent Meadow. Continue straight ahead past the Huckleberry Meadow junction (3.2 miles/5.2 km), and when you reach the second junction with trails leading east along the north side of Crescent Meadow, make a left turn on the second of those two trails. This second trail will circumnavigate the east edge of Crescent Meadow before returning to the Crescent Meadow parking area at 4 miles (6.4 km).

18   CRESCENT AND LOG MEADOWS

Distance: 2.1 miles (3.4 km)
Elevation gain: 200 feet (60 m)
High point: 6857 feet (2090 m)
Difficulty: Easy
Trail surface: Dirt
Map: USGS 7.5-min Giant Forest
GPS: 36.554855°, -118.749003°
Notes: Day use only; good for kids; restroom at the trailhead; winter snowshoeing route

> This easy loop visits the two largest and arguably most beautiful of Giant Forest's numerous meadows. Called the "gem of the Sierra" by that noted waxer of poetics, John Muir, Crescent Meadow is an essential stopping point for all Giant Forest visitors. Rivaling Crescent Meadow in beauty, adjacent Log Meadow, so named due to the presence of Hale Tharp's cabin built from a sequoia, rounds off this memorable Giant Forest experience.

GETTING THERE

Driving: From the Ash Mountain Entrance, drive north for 16.4 miles (26.4 km) along winding Generals Highway, and turn right onto Crescent Meadow Road. Continue for 1.2 miles (1.9 km) to a junction with Moro Rock Road and make a slight left to stay on Crescent Meadow Road. After another 1.3 miles (2.1 km), the road terminates at the Crescent Meadow/High Sierra Trailhead.

Transit: Gray Route 2 stops at Crescent Meadow. Note that the park may close Crescent Meadow Road to automobile traffic during the peak season (mid-May to mid-September), during which time the shuttle is the only way to access the trailhead.

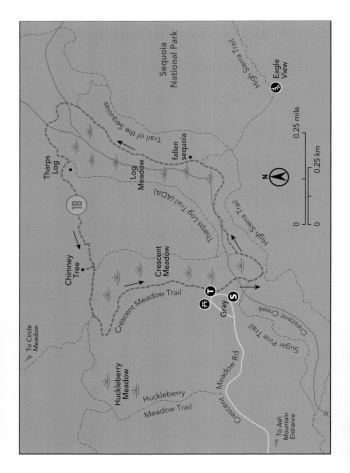

ON THE TRAIL

From the combined Crescent Meadow and High Sierra Trailhead on the east end of the Crescent Meadow parking lot, head south and then east around the southern tip of Crescent Meadow via a paved trail. Keep left at two successive junctions with one branch of the Sugar Pine Trail and then the

High Sierra Trail. After 0.2 mile (0.3 km), the trail approaches the edge of Crescent Meadow, where a wooden sign proclaims it the "gem of the Sierra." From this viewpoint, Crescent Meadow unfurls across a sunny, open space bounded on all sides by towering sequoias.

After the "gem of the Sierra" sign, continue a short distance to a trail leading to Log Meadow. Turn right onto this trail, leaving the pavement behind. Follow the trail east as it parallels the south bank of Crescent Creek on a mild incline toward the southern tip of Log Meadow. At 0.5 mile (0.8 km), keep left at a junction with a connecting trail that climbs to a junction with the Trail of the Sequoias and the High Sierra Trail. Just beyond this junction, look for a massive fallen sequoia that elicits a renewed appreciation for just how big the trees are.

Continue north along the eastern edge of the meadow, and keep left once again at 0.9 mile (1.4 km) at a junction with

Crescent Meadow bathed in evening light

another connector trail accessing the Trail of the Sequoias. Beyond this connector trail, the trail arcs around the northern edge of the meadow to approach Tharps Log. You reach Hale Tharp's humble abode 1.2 miles (1.9 km) from the start and just south of a junction with a trail leading west toward the Chimney Tree and Crescent Meadow. After admiring both Tharp's ingenuity and the beauty of Log Meadow, backtrack to this junction and head west toward Crescent Meadow.

At 1.5 miles (2.4 km), take a short detour on a spur trail that leads north toward the Chimney Tree, a still-vertical dead sequoia hollowed out by fire. You can crawl into the Chimney Tree and look up through the cavity in the top of the trunk—a not-so-subtle clue as to why it's called the Chimney Tree.

Backtrack from the Chimney Tree and resume your westward travel toward a junction with a trail that heads south along the eastern edge of Crescent Meadow. Keep right at that junction and continue toward a junction with a trail that leads south along the western edge of the meadow at 1.7 miles (2.7 km). Turn left here, and follow the trail south. You will reach the Crescent Meadow parking area at 2.1 miles (3.4 km).

19 TRAIL OF THE SEQUOIAS

Distance: 6 miles (9.7 km)
Elevation gain: 1200 feet (370 m)
High point: 7354 feet (2241 m)
Difficulty: Challenging
Trail surface: Dirt
Map: USGS 7.5-min Giant Forest
GPS: 36.554855°, -118.749003°
Notes: Day use only; restroom at the trailhead; winter snowshoeing route

One of the miracles of hiking in Giant Forest is that no matter how many people you encounter at each of the four staging areas, if you walk half a mile along any given trail, you will have the forest to yourself. The lightly traveled Trail of the Sequoias epitomizes this phenomenon while following a peaceful track to a number of famous and lesser-known Giant Forest highlights. This challenging but satisfying journey is one of the best ways to get to know Giant Forest beyond the various roadside attractions that draw so much visitor attention.

GETTING THERE

Driving: From the Ash Mountain Entrance, drive north for 16.4 miles (26.4 km) along winding Generals Highway, and turn right onto Crescent Meadow Road. Continue for 1.2 miles (1.9 km) to a junction with Moro Rock Road and make a slight left to stay on Crescent Meadow Road. After another 1.3 miles (2.1 km), the road terminates at the Crescent Meadow/High Sierra Trailhead.

Transit: Gray Route 2 stops at Crescent Meadow. Note that the park may close Crescent Meadow Road to automobile traffic during the peak season (mid-May to mid-September), during which time the shuttle is the only way to access the trailhead.

ON THE TRAIL

Starting from the Crescent Meadow staging area, join the paved High Sierra Trail (known as the HST) and follow it 350 yards (300 m) south to a junction where the now unpaved HST diverges on the right. Continue following the HST through a pure stand of white firs rising from a picturesque carpet of ferns and lupines toward the southern crest of the Giant Forest plateau. At 0.5 mile (0.8 km), you will reach a four-way junction with two trails branching off on the left.

For an impressive view of Middle Fork Kaweah Canyon, veer right on the HST and continue 0.2 mile (0.3 km) southeast to Eagle View. This viewpoint affords a spacious panorama of the canyon and the lofty peaks of the Great Western Divide.

Retrace your steps back to the four-way junction, and turn right on the Trail of the Sequoias. As you progress, the trail traverses a heavily forested hillside carpeted with ferns about 200 feet (60 m) above Log Meadow. As the trail peels away from a junction connecting to Log Meadow, it con- tours into and out of a pair of idyllic ravines at 1.6 miles (2.6 km) and 2.6 miles (4.2 km). Within these two ravines, the

Ferns and firs greet hikers on the opening segment of the fabled High Sierra Trail.

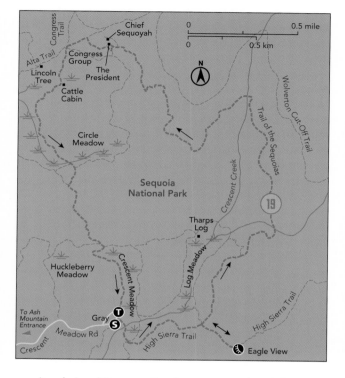

gurgling forks of Crescent Creek carry water downhill to feed Crescent and Log Meadows.

After the second ravine, the trail makes a hairpin turn to ascend a sunny, rocky ridge. The vegetation on the south-facing slope of this ridge tends toward more drought-tolerant Jeffrey pine, manzanita, and mountain misery, although a towering, gnarled sequoia draws immediate attention on the center of the ridge. This gnarled specimen marks the high point for the route. From here, it's a leisurely downhill stroll that passes by a number of notable highlights in the heart of the grove.

At 3.9 miles (6.3 km), the Trail of the Sequoias passes a junction with connecting trails leading north to the Alta Trail and south to the Circle Meadow Trail. Continue straight until the Trail of the Sequoias terminates at the Congress Trail in the shade of the President and Chief Sequoyah Trees. From here, turn left and continue due south to follow the Circle Meadow Loop Trail along the western and then southern segments of Circle Meadow. At 5 miles (8 km), veer to the left to follow the Crescent Meadow Trail south toward Crescent Meadow and its adjacent parking area. As you traverse the western edge of Crescent Meadow, keep your eyes peeled for black bears, marmots, and mule deer browsing for succulent morsels in the meadow's rich habitat.

20 CONGRESS TRAIL

Distance: 2.8 miles (4.5 km)
Elevation gain: 500 feet (150 m)
High point: 7079 feet (2158 m)
Difficulty: Moderate
Trail surface: Paved
Map: USGS 7.5-min Giant Forest
GPS: 36.584783°, -118.749781°
Notes: Day use only; good for kids; ADA accessible; restroom at trailhead

If you have time for only one hike on your visit to Giant Forest, this is, without a doubt, the one to take. The Congress Trail visits the largest and most famous of the giant sequoias, the General Sherman Tree, before penetrating the heart of Giant Forest to witness other impressive highlights within the grove. Wildlife sightings, including black bears, mule deer, marmots, and a host of small mammals and birds, are common, especially in the mornings and evenings.

The General Sherman Tree is a giant among giants.

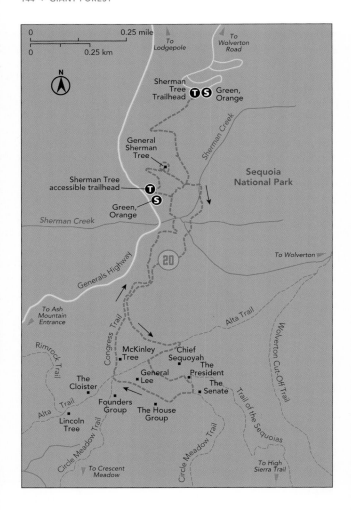

GETTING THERE

Driving: From the Ash Mountain Entrance, head north on Generals Highway for 19.1 miles (30.7 km) to an intersection with Wolverton Road. Turn right and continue for 0.6 mile (1 km) to another intersection signed for General Sherman parking. Turn right again and continue for another 0.6 mile (1 km) to park at the signed Sherman Tree Trailhead. The Giant Forest accessible trail, at which only vehicles with disability placards may park, lies 0.6 mile (1 km) south from the Wolverton Road junction.

Transit: Both Green Route 1 and Orange Route 4 stop at the General Sherman accessible trail stop and the General Sherman Tree main trail.

ON THE TRAIL

From either trailhead, follow the signed and paved path toward the General Sherman Tree, which will be difficult to miss due to the crowds congregating around the base. If you're starting from the accessible trailhead, this is a short 0.1-mile (0.2-km) walk. From the main trail parking area, it's a 0.4-mile (0.6-km) walk that loses about 200 feet (60 m) of elevation. The Sherman Tree attains the greatest size, measured by volume, of any single living tree, and its height of 275 feet (85-m), weight of 4.2 million pounds (1.9 million kg), and estimated age between 2300 and 2700 years represent numeric descriptions that stand firmly outside comprehension.

A surprisingly large percentage of visitors stop at the Sherman Tree and go no farther, but Giant Forest won't reveal the extent of its wonders if you only hang around the Sherman Tree. From the Sherman Tree, head east toward the signed trailhead for the Congress Trail. Step onto the paved trail and immediately cross Sherman Creek on a small wooden bridge before traversing a hillside studded with massive sequoias. A handful of paths connect the east and west branches of the Congress Trail, allowing hikers to cut their trips short if necessary.

At 0.5 mile (0.8 km) from the Sherman Tree, the Congress Trail climbs gently over a low ridge to reach an impressive group of trees in the heart of Giant Forest, clustered around a junction with the Alta Trail. Turn right for a short stretch on the Alta Trail, and make an immediate left to return to the Congress Trail as it loops past the Senate and House Groups. Keep right at junctions for the Trail of the Sequoias and the Circle Meadow Loop Trail, and continue toward a five-way junction marked by a kiosk displaying a map of Giant Forest. The Alta Trail, return branch of the Congress Trail, and a spur trail to the McKinley Tree meet at this junction, presenting a wealth of options for extended travel.

The monikers of individual and copses of trees reflect the tradition of naming sequoias after venerable institutions and historic figures. Most of the named trees are exceptional in terms of size, age, and height. Chief among these trees is the President, which rivals the Sherman and the Grant Trees as the third-largest sequoia. With a little exploration, you will also find the Chief Sequoyah Tree situated slightly to the northwest of the President; the General Lee Tree; the Lincoln Tree, a short distance south on the Alta Trail; the McKinley Tree, a short distance northeast from the five-way junction; and the aforementioned House, Senate, and Founders Groups.

From the five-way junction, stay straight to head due north along the Congress Trail as it returns to the General Sherman Tree. From the Sherman Tree, follow the access trail back up the hill to the parking area north of the tree, or walk back to Generals Highway to catch the shuttle to your next destination.

GOING FARTHER

From the five-way junction with the Alta Trail, there are countless options for exploring Giant Forest. Specific recommendations might include looping around Circle Meadow (Route

17), continuing south to Crescent Meadow (Route 18) and taking a shuttle back, turning left on the Alta Trail and following it to Wolverton (Route 21), following the Trail of the Sequoias (Route 19) to the High Sierra Trail, and connecting with the Rimrock Trail and following it to Giant Forest Museum.

WOLVERTON, LODGEPOLE, AND DORST CREEK

For much of the park's early history, visitor services spread throughout Giant Forest, leading to a slow degradation of the habitat and a recognition that more would need to be done to protect the big trees. In response to this degradation, park administrators relocated these facilities into less sensitive habitats, creating four major hubs of activity containing the bulk of the park's visitor services. These four hubs, including Wolverton, Lodgepole, Wuksachi Lodge, and Dorst Creek, contain a number of trailheads accessing mixed-conifer forest, sequoia groves, alpine summits, and lake basins.

The Wolverton area provides the primary access point to the Alta and Lakes Trails that penetrate the high country east of Giant Forest. Situated along Long Meadow, Wolverton contains a shuttle stop, a picnic area, and it often hosts a summertime barbeque that attracts hungry visitors. During winter, Wolverton transforms into a snow-play area to the delight of visiting families.

Lodgepole contains a pair of trailheads, including the popular Tokopah Valley Trail that departs from Lodgepole Campground on its way to Tokopah Falls, Sequoia's largest waterfall. Lodgepole also contains the park's second-largest campground, a visitor center and ranger station, a market, laundromat, shuttle stops, picnic areas, and a café. With all

OPPOSITE: *The smaller of the Twin Lakes with Twin Peaks setting the backdrop (Route 25)*

of these facilities, Lodgepole often becomes a fairly hectic place. However, Lodgepole Campground's location makes it an ideal base camp for exploring the Giant Forest area.

Additional lodging can be found at the luxurious Wuksachi Lodge located just north of Lodgepole. A second sprawling campground at Dorst Creek accommodates visitors during the busier summer season. Dorst Campground also contains a single trailhead for the Muir Grove Trail, which departs from the campground's western edge.

The Sequoia Shuttle services all four of these hubs. Orange Route 4 is the only shuttle that reaches Wolverton, and it connects Wolverton to the General Sherman Trailheads. Green Route 1 runs from Lodgepole to Giant Forest Museum, with stops at both General Sherman Trailheads. Purple Route 3 runs between Lodgepole and Dorst Creek, with stops at Lodgepole Campground, the Lodgepole Visitor Center, Wuksachi Lodge, and Dorst Creek Campground.

21 WOLVERTON TO GIANT FOREST MUSEUM

Distance: 5.4 miles (8.7 km)
Elevation gain: 500 feet (150 m)
High point: 7233 feet (2205 m)
Difficulty: Moderate
Trail surface: Dirt, with two short sections of pavement
Maps: USGS 7.5-min Lodgepole, Giant Forest
GPS: 36.596632°, -118.734391°
Notes: Day use only; restrooms available at Wolverton and Giant Forest Museum

Thanks to the combination of an extensive trail network connecting Wolverton to the Giant Forest Museum and the convenience of the Sequoia Shuttle, visitors to the area can craft a number of point-to-point routes that take in a variety of highlights in and around Giant Forest. One such route skirts the eastern edge of Long Meadow just south of Wolverton before joining with the Alta Trail for a stroll through the length of Giant Forest. This mostly downhill route visits corners of Giant Forest that few visitors ever experience while still stopping off at some of the most famous highlights.

The Alta Trail traverses a quiet corner of Giant Forest.

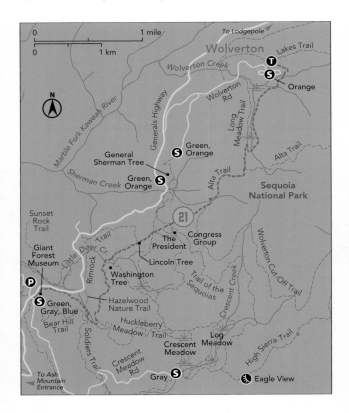

GETTING THERE

Combined Driving and Transit Instructions: From the Ash Mountain Entrance, head north on Generals Highway for 16.4 miles (26.4 km) to the parking area for the Giant Forest Museum. Leave your car parked at the Giant Forest Museum and take Green Route 1 to the General Sherman Tree parking area. From there, take Orange Route 4 to Wolverton. Walk to the northeast corner of the parking area to find the Lakes Trailhead. From here, you will walk back to your car at the Giant Forest Museum.

ON THE TRAIL

After locating the Lakes Trailhead, head north on a short spur trail that leads to a junction with the Lakes Trail heading east and a trail traveling to Lodgepole leading west. Turn right at this junction, and then make an immediate right turn on a trail signed for the Long Meadow Loop. Follow this trail downhill as it loops around some buildings on its way to an unimproved crossing of Wolverton Creek at 0.5 mile (0.8 km). If you're hiking during the early part of the season (May and June), you may have to wade carefully across Wolverton Creek. Later in the season, this is an easy crossing over rocks and logs.

Once past the creek, continue through an initially dense patch of forest before emerging upon a sunny meadow. At 0.9 mile (1.4 km), the trail reaches the edge of Long Meadow, which occupies the marshy ground between two rocky slopes. The trail travels south along the east edge of the meadow until it switchbacks to higher ground to avoid some swampy terrain at the meadow's inlet. After crossing the inlet, the trail reaches a junction with the return branch of the Long Meadow Trail at 1.6 miles (2.6 km). If you want a shorter hike, you can turn right to follow the Long Meadow Trail back to Wolverton Road. If you want sequoias, turn left and begin a short, but steep ascent up and over a saddle due south from the junction.

After cresting the saddle, the trail drops a short distance to a junction with the Alta Trail. Turn right on the Alta Trail, and begin a long downhill stroll toward the Giant Forest Museum. Although you pass numerous junctions between the first junction and the museum, only the Wolverton Cut-Off Trail Junction at 2.6 miles (4.2 km) creates confusion. The confusion is the result of dense thickets of ferns and lupines, which can obscure the trail signs. Avoid turning left, which will put you on the Wolverton Cut-Off Trail. If you find yourself climbing a hillside, turn back as that means you ended up going the wrong way. Remain on the Alta Trail to travel southwest on a pleasant, downhill grade.

As you continue past the Wolverton Cut-Off junction, the Alta Trail passes through quiet sequoia forest that seldom receives visitors. This tranquility is broken when the Alta Trail reaches a junction with the Congress Trail at 3.1 miles (5 km). The Alta Trail becomes paved at this point and runs concurrently with the Congress Trail briefly before the two trails diverge. Continue straight to remain on the Alta Trail and follow it to a five-way junction at 3.25 miles (5.2 km). This junction features a kiosk containing a map of Giant Forest, which can help you get your bearings if you're feeling a little confused about what is where.

Continue straight on the Alta Trail toward the Giant Forest Museum. The pavement disappears shortly after the junction, and you pass the towering Lincoln Tree at 3.3 miles (5.3 km). Continue straight at a junction with the Rimrock Trail at 3.4 miles (5.4 km). After the Rimrock Trail, continue straight past a junction leading to the Washington Tree at 3.7 miles (6 km). Just beyond this junction, the Alta Trail crosses Little Deer Creek and a copse of quaking aspen trees. On the other side of a wooden bridge spanning the creek, look to the right for a sign indicating the presence of bedrock mortars. The indigenous peoples of the region used these mortars to process seeds and acorns to create meal that they made into cakes and porridges.

Beyond the mortars, the Alta Trail bends south as it descends across a sequoia-studded hillside toward a tributary of Little Deer Creek. Stay straight at the junction with the Huckleberry Meadow Trail on your left at 4.4 miles (7.1 km). After crossing the creek and making a sharp bend to the northwest, continue straight at a junction for the Bear Hill and Soldiers Trails at 4.7 miles (7.6 km). Stay straight at two more junctions with the Hazelwood Nature Trail Loop at 4.8 and 5 miles (7.7 and 8 km). Continue straight at a junction for the Big Trees Trail at 5.1 miles (8.2 km) and again with another leg of the Bear Hill Trail at 5.2 miles (8.4 km). The Alta Trail comes to its conclusion just east of the Giant Forest Museum, 5.4 miles (8.7 km) from where you started at Wolverton.

GOING FARTHER

If you want to get even more solitude and some killer views of the Great Western Divide served up with a segment of the historic High Sierra Trail, you can turn left onto the Wolverton Cut-Off Trail at the 2.6-mile (4.2-km) junction. This quiet footpath leads south, paralleling the Trail of the Sequoias, before descending from a jaw-dropping viewpoint to the High Sierra Trail. Turn right onto the High Sierra Trail, which will take you back to Crescent Meadow for a 9.2-mile (14.2-km) odyssey that gains 1400 feet (425 km) of elevation. Note that you will need to add one more shuttle—Gray Route 2—to reach the Giant Forest Museum from Crescent Meadow.

22 ALTA PEAK

Distance: 13.2 miles (21.2 km)
Elevation gain: 4200 feet (1280 m)
High point: 11,204 feet (3415 m)
Difficulty: Strenuous
Trail surface: Dirt, with some sand near the summit
Map: USGS 7.5-min Lodgepole
GPS: 36.596632°, -118.734391°
Notes: Suitable for backpacking; restroom near the trailhead

Strap on your packs and lace up your boots for a tough, unforgettable journey to the summit of Alta Peak. From this 11,204-foot (3415-m) high point, you will experience jaw-dropping views spanning the terrain from Three Rivers all the way to

Mount Whitney—an elevation range of nearly 13,500 feet (4115 m). Views of the glaciated ramparts of the Great Western Divide receding into the yawning chasm of the Middle Fork Kaweah River canyon contrast with the more intimate pleasures of a grove of ancient foxtail pines, a pair of tranquil meadows, and a gloriously high rate of calorie incineration.

GETTING THERE

Driving: From the Ash Mountain Entrance, continue north on Generals Highway for 19.1 miles (30.7 km) to Wolverton Road. Turn right and follow Wolverton Road for 1.4 miles (2.3 km), and make a left into a parking area for the combined Alta Peak/Lakes Trailhead.

Transit: Orange Route 4 runs between the two General Sherman Trailheads and Wolverton.

ON THE TRAIL

From the combined Alta Peak/Lakes Trail staging area, head due north and turn right almost immediately at a T junction with the Lakes Trail heading east and a trail leading west to Lodgepole. Stay straight on the Lakes Trail at the immediate junction with the Long Meadow Trail. Commence a moderate climb along the ridge dividing Wolverton from Tokopah Valley through a dense forest of red fir. Wolverton Creek trickles along on your right, sometimes a few hundred feet downslope and sometimes only a few dozen feet away. Cross a colorful, spring-fed meadow with seasonal streams and wildflowers before reaching a junction at 1.8 miles (2.9 km). The Lakes Trail heads left but keep right to continue southeast on the Panther Gap Trail.

At 2.8 miles (4.5 km), you reach Panther Gap, where you get your first glimpse south of the gaping chasm of Middle Fork Kaweah River canyon yawning impressively to the south. The distinctive Castle Rocks protrude from thickly forested Paradise Ridge directly south across the canyon, while

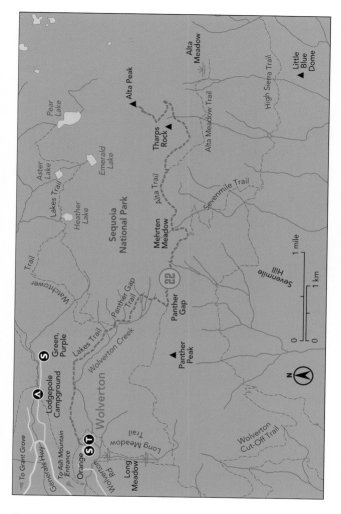

the crags and spires of the Great Western Divide emerge into view for the first time. Turn left onto the Alta Trail, heading due east. Keep your eyes peeled for a large granitic rock

The Kaweah Peaks crown the ramparts of the Great Western Divide.

outcrop that resembles the head of a grizzly bear at the 3.1-mile (5-km) mark.

At 4 miles (6.4 km), the trail dips into a shaded ravine with Mehrten Meadow slanting downhill. Mehrten Meadow offers the first of two possible camping areas (no food storage) if you are taking this route as an overnight hike. Beyond Mehrten Meadow, the trail climbs at a moderate rate toward a junction with the Alta Meadow Trail. At this junction, a spur trail that heads east for 1.1 miles (1.8 km) to Alta Meadow continues on the right. Alta Meadow is the second of two possible camping areas on this route (also no food storage), and for hikers who run out of steam on their way to the peak, the meadow is a great consolation prize with stellar views of the Great Western Divide.

From the Alta Meadow junction, turn left to cross the spring-fed creek, which tumbles down a wide, rocky ravine leading downhill from Alta Peak. The trail becomes noticeably steeper as it gains 1000 feet (300 m) per mile over the next 2 miles (3.2 km) to the summit. The elevation above 9000 feet (2740 m) is where most people begin to feel the effects of diminished oxygen in the high-altitude atmosphere, so the slow going may become even slower as you try to keep up with your breath. The trail continues east along the southern base of Tharps Rock before the trail makes a pronounced switchback to the west. Beyond this switchback lies a grove of foxtail pines, a subalpine species that typically thrives on the drier, eastern side of the Sierra Nevada. Foxtails live up to three thousand years, and they attain a gnarled and twisted appearance as they age.

After a short 0.2 mile (0.3 km) of walking through the foxtail pines, tree species surrender completely to the merciless alpine conditions near the summit. As you pass the tree line, only small ground-hugging plants can tolerate the cold winters and short summers. Diligent, patient effort will place you at the base of Alta Peak's summit block, which you can climb to obtain the true summit.

The summit views are nothing short of extraordinary. The full extent of Middle Fork Kaweah River canyon unfurls before you as the towering peaks of the Great Western Divide take on greater detail and relief due to proximity. To the north, upper Tokopah Valley rises up to Alta Peak's sister summit, Mount Silliman, while the Kings Canyon high country shimmers in the distance. Eagle-eyed observers will be able to spot Mount Whitney through a gap in the Great Western Divide. Allow yourself at least an hour to enjoy this scene before beginning the long downhill trek back to Wolverton.

23 LAKES TRAIL

Distance: 12.2 miles (19.6 km)
Elevation gain: 2700 feet (820 m)
High point: 9567 feet (2916 m)
Difficulty: Strenuous
Trail surface: Dirt, with occasionally rocky stretches
Maps: USGS 7.5-min Lodgepole
GPS: 36.596632°, -118.734391°
Notes: Suitable for backpacking; restroom adjacent to trailhead; restrooms also available at Emerald Lake and Pear Lake

Although Sequoia National Park contains a wealth of shimmering lakes, glacial basins, and memorable vistas, many of those destinations are accessible only via multiday backcountry excursions. One of the notable exceptions to this general rule—the Lakes Trail—sets out from Wolverton to reach a quartet of subalpine lakes nestled in glacial basins on the north slopes of Alta Peak. Hikers can tackle this strenuous route either as an ambitious day hike or as an overnight hike with camping options at Emerald and Pear Lakes.

GETTING THERE

Driving: From the Ash Mountain Entrance, continue 19.1 miles (30.7 km) to Wolverton Road. Turn right and follow Wolverton Road for 1.4 miles (2.3 km), and make a left into a parking area for the Lakes Trailhead.

Transit: Orange Route 4 runs from the Sherman Tree accessible trailhead to Wolverton.

ON THE TRAIL

Hikers looking to follow this route as an overnight backpacking trip must obtain a permit in advance. Unlike every other backcountry trailhead in Sequoia and Kings Canyon

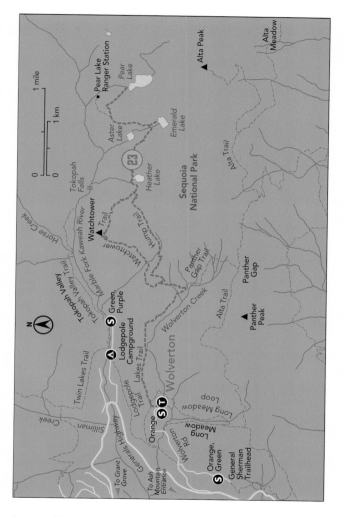

National Parks, the Lakes Trail permits are available only on a first-come, first-served basis at the Lodgepole Visitor Center. Given the high demand for permits, your best strategy will be to arrive at the visitor center early, preferably when the center opens. The odds are always in the early bird's favor.

The Lakes Trail begins from the northeastern corner of Wolverton's parking area. Start by following a short spur trail north to a junction with the Lakes Trail leading right (east) and a trail descending to Lodgepole leading left. Turn right onto the Lakes Trail, and continue past the junction for the Long Meadow Trail. After these junctions, settle in for a moderate ascent through a dense forest composed primarily of red fir. At 0.8 mile (1.3 km), the trail sidles up to Wolverton Creek at a point where it fuels a small meadow. Hikers who get an early start may spot bears browsing for food over the next 0.2 mile (0.3 km).

After the meadow, the trail bends to the southeast to continue climbing to a junction with the Panther Gap Trail at 1.8 miles (2.9 km). Turn left at this junction to continue climbing along the Lakes Trail. After 0.3 mile (0.5 km) of climbing, the trail arrives at a junction where the Lakes Trail splits into the Watchtower Trail and the Hump Trail. The Watchtower Trail is the more scenic of the two, as it skirts the rim of Tokopah Valley past the Watchtower. However, several sections of the trail between the Watchtower and Heather Lake cling to a precipitous cliffside that becomes lethal when ice and snow are present. If ice and snow are present, as is possible from any time between October and July, the park keeps this section of the trail closed, thus obliging you to follow the less scenic but more direct Hump Trail.

Assuming the Watchtower Trail is open, turn left, and continue climbing toward the rim of Tokopah Valley. The trail remains under heavy tree cover until 3.2 miles (5.2 km), at which point a short section of switchbacks brings you to the Watchtower. The Watchtower heralds a transition from pleasant forest walking to stunning alpine scenery. Mount Silliman's towering massif looms directly across Tokopah Valley, and once you climb past the Watchtower, you will be able to

Emerald Lake's still waters reflecting Alta Peak

spot the upper reaches of Tokopah Falls where the Marble Fork Kaweah River roars over a thousand feet into the valley below. As mentioned before, the trail beyond the Watchtower clings to the side of a precipitous cliff before reaching a grove of lodgepole and Western white pines that heralds your arrival at Heather Lake at 4.1 miles (6.6 km).

Heather Lake, so named because of copious growths of heather along the banks, nestles snugly into a partially wooded basin. The park forbids camping along the banks to curb overuse and protect habitat. With the worst of the climb behind you, Heather Lake is an optimal place to rest for a spell before continuing on to the next three lakes.

Cross Heather Lake's outlet, and begin a switchbacking ascent up and over the ridge dividing Heather Lake's basin from the Aster and Emerald Lakes basin to the east. Once on the east side of the ridge, you will get your first look at Aster Lake. The Lakes Trail doesn't reach Aster Lake, but you can work your way across granite slabs to reach the shore. The trail continues past Aster Lake on a 200-foot (60-m) descent toward the outlet of Emerald Lake. Ten separate campsites cluster around a grove of trees near the lake's outlet. To reach the shore of Emerald Lake, follow the path south through the camping area until it ends at the lake. The basin containing Emerald Lake rises up nearly 2000 feet (610 m) to the summit of Alta Peak due southeast, adding a punctuation mark to a classic scene of High Sierra beauty.

Pear Lake, the final and easily most beautiful lake, lies in the next basin to the east. To reach it, the Lakes Trail wraps around the ridge separating the two basins. Keep right at the spur trail leading left toward the Pear Lake Ranger Station (5.6 miles/9 km), and continue on a moderate ascent to the banks of the lake. Several campsites lie on outcrops surrounding the south shore of the lake. Large slabs of granite near the lake's outlet provide great spots to relax and repose beneath brilliant Sierran sunshine. If you are day hiking, be sure to budget at least one hour (preferably two) so that you have plenty of time to explore, as you will have an extremely difficult time turning your back on Pear Lake.

24 TOKOPAH FALLS

Distance: 3.8 miles (6.1 km)
Elevation gain: 600 feet (180 m)
High point: 7405 feet (2257 m)

Difficulty: Moderate
Trail surface: Dirt, with rocky sections at the end
Map: USGS 7.5-min Lodgepole
GPS: 36.605216°, -118.722690°
Notes: Day use only; good for kids; restrooms adjacent to the trailhead

From its birthplace high along the Kings-Kaweah Divide in the Tablelands region, the Marble Fork Kaweah River collects prodigious amounts of snowmelt from the high country before thundering 1200 feet (365 m) into Tokopah Valley. Once it reaches the valley's gently sloping floor, the Marble Fork's crystalline waters meander through a dense forest before rushing past the central hub of Lodgepole. This family-friendly hike takes in all of the moods of the Marble Fork while adding a generous dose of tranquil forest and a good likelihood of wildlife sightings.

GETTING THERE

Driving: From the Ash Mountain Entrance, continue 21.9 miles (35.2 km) on Generals Highway to Lodgepole Road. Turn right, pass the village of Lodgepole, then pass through the Lodgepole Campground entrance to reach a large lot open to day hikers. Park here and walk across the bridge spanning the river. The Tokopah Valley Trail lies on the right just beyond the bridge.

Transit: Purple Line 3 connects Lodgepole Campground with Wuksachi and Dorst Creek. Green Line 1 connects Lodgepole Campground with both General Sherman Tree Trailheads and the Giant Forest Museum.

ON THE TRAIL

Join the Tokopah Valley Trail and begin hiking east as the trail passes through a pleasing assortment of mixed-conifer forest, occasional granite outcrops, and early summer flower

The lower cascades of Tokopah Falls

fields composed of yellow-throated gilia. The Marble Fork rumbles along on your right, and for the first 0.4 mile (0.6 km), you will also spot colorful tents giving away the location of campsites on Lodgepole Campground's eastern margins. Side paths lead down to the river, but the rapid current of the river coupled with its low temperature make it dangerous for swimming.

After the trail leaves the campground behind, it passes through an assortment of highlights as it travels toward Tokopah Falls. Views toward the Watchtower, a granite monolith resembling a lookout that rises nearly 2000 feet (600 m) above the valley floor, open up at various points where the trail follows bends in the river. Black bears may be found frolicking in pocket meadows nourished by spring-fed streams. A mixture of cedars, pines, firs, and black oaks cast shade along the trail, keeping hikers cool and comfortable as they progress along the trail's gentle uphill grade.

After passing an unnamed creek (at 1.25 miles/2 km) shortly followed by Horse Creek (at 1.3 miles/2.1 km), the

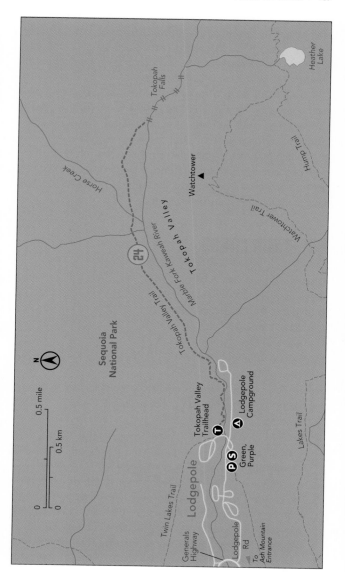

Heather Lake

Tokopah Falls

Hump Trail

Horse Creek

Watchtower

Watchtower Trail

Tokopah Valley

Marble Fork Kaweah River

Tokopah Valley Trail

Sequoia National Park

N

0.5 mile

0.5 km

Twin Lakes Trail

Lodgepole

Tokopah Valley Trailhead

T

Lodgepole Campground

A

P S

Green, Purple

Lakes Trail

Generals Highway

Lodgepole Rd

To Ash Mountain Entrance

trail makes its final approach toward Tokopah Falls. The falls will be visible through gaps in leafy black oaks. At 1.7 miles (2.7 km), the trail leaves tree cover to enter a granite amphitheater into which roars Tokopah Falls.

Continue through a rocky stretch of trail populated by a lively group of marmots until reaching its end at the base of the falls. From this vantage, you can't see the upper reaches of the cascading waterfall, but the lower 200 feet (60 m) of the falls are quite spectacular on their own. Note that the flow of the river dwindles as summer progresses, and visitors arriving any time from August through early November may find the falls almost completely dry.

25 TWIN LAKES

Distance: 13.6 miles (21.9 km)
Elevation gain: 3000 feet (915 m)
High point: 9446 feet (2879 m)
Difficulty: Strenuous
Trail surface: Dirt
Map: USGS 7.5-min Lodgepole
GPS: 36.605216°, -118.722690°
Notes: Suitable for backpacking; food storage lockers at camping areas; restrooms adjacent to the trailhead

Perched in the shadow of the Kings-Kaweah Divide, Twin Lakes provides a road-accessible day-hiking option to reach scenery usually reserved for backpackers. Although the lakes are really only twins in the fraternal sense, the destination on the end of this long and satisfying out-and-back trip yields a ton of scenic beauty. This popular hike doubles as a great backpacking experience, and regularly spaced highlights including creek crossings, sprawling meadows, and serene subalpine forests round out a satisfying hiking experience.

GETTING THERE

Driving: From the Ash Mountain Entrance, continue 21.9 miles (35.2 km) on Generals Highway to Lodgepole Road. Turn right, pass the village of Lodgepole, then pass through the Lodgepole Campground entrance to reach a large lot open to day hikers. Park here and walk across the bridge spanning the river. The Twin Lakes Trail lies on the right just beyond the bridge.

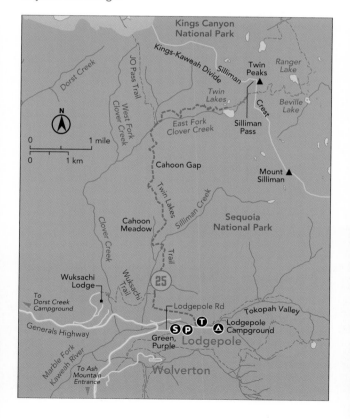

Transit: Purple Line 3 connects Lodgepole Campground with Wuksachi and Dorst Creek. Green Line 1 connects Lodgepole Campground with both General Sherman Tree Trailheads and the Giant Forest Museum.

ON THE TRAIL

Follow the Twin Lakes Trail as it curves behind a set of campsites before beginning an oblique climb along Tokopah Valley's northern wall. After ascending through dry mixed-conifer forest, the trees transition into an oppressively dense forest of red fir and lodgepole pines at 1 mile (1.6 km). From here, the trail turns due north, continuing through the red fir–lodgepole forest toward a junction with the Wuksachi Trail at 1.1 miles (1.8 km). At 2.2 miles (3.5 km), carefully work your way across Silliman Creek while avoiding any direct contact with the water; this creek supplies the water for the Lodgepole area, and the humans residing downstream don't appreciate any special additives to their drinking water.

After crossing Silliman Creek, the trail crosses a wooded ridge before dropping down to the edge of Cahoon Meadow

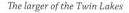

The larger of the Twin Lakes

at 2.6 miles (4.2 km), which occupies about an American football field's worth of flat sylvan terrain. The climb resumes shortly beyond the meadow through more dense forest before cresting at Cahoon Gap at 4.2 miles (6.8 km). After cresting the gap, you lose a dispiriting 250 feet (75 m) that you will have to regain on the return journey.

After bottoming out at a tributary to Clover Creek, look to the right for a food storage locker indicating possible campsites. Resume climbing en route to a junction with the JO Pass Trail at 5.2 miles (8.3 km), which features another locker and campsites alongside the banks of the East Fork Clover Creek. Turn right to begin switchbacking in a generally eastern direction over rocky slopes on the north banks of the creek. A series of cascades provide interest at a handful of spots where the trail nears the creek.

At 6.7 miles (10.8 km), the terrain flattens out upon reaching a rocky, wooded isthmus separating the two lakes. The northern lake is the smaller and marshier of the two. Despite the more diminutive size, this lake also features great views of Twin Peaks. The southern lake is much larger and features a more classic High Sierra lake appearance. A pair of food storage lockers service a sprawling set of campsites. Be sure to stick to the designated sites and avoid making new ones. The established campsites help to ensure that overuse does not become a bigger problem than it already is.

GOING FARTHER

If you are backpacking, you can enjoy a gorgeous extension of the route that climbs up and over Silliman Pass (7.9 miles/12.7 km) before descending to Beville and Ranger Lakes (9.6 miles/15.5 km and 9.9 miles/15.9 km, respectively). Ranger Lake has a food storage locker and numerous campsites. Nearby views into Sugarloaf Valley and along the Kings-Kaweah Divide are outstanding.

26 LITTLE BALDY

Distance: 3.4 miles (5.5 km)
Elevation gain: 800 feet (240 m)
High point: 8044 feet (2452 m)
Difficulty: Moderate
Trail surface: Dirt
Map: USGS 7.5-min Giant Forest
GPS: 36.620071°, -118.809216°
Notes: Day use only; good for kids; no restroom at trailhead

> High atop a forested ridge dividing the Marble and North Forks of the Kaweah River, a rounded granite dome protrudes from the tree cover like a medieval monk's bald spot. This spot has earned the moniker "Little Baldy," and the comfortable rounded summit serves up sweeping panoramic views that take in the Sequoia foothills, the Silliman Crest, and the Great Western Divide. The route is easy enough for older kids as well, who may appreciate the combination of fun exploration on the summit coupled with outstanding vistas.

GETTING THERE

From the Ash Mountain Entrance, continue 27.8 miles (44.7 km) on Generals Highway, passing the village of Lodgepole, to arrive at the Little Baldy Trailhead. There is roadside parking on either side of Generals Highway.

ON THE TRAIL

From Little Baldy Saddle, find the trailhead on the east side of the road and follow the trail as it gains some quick elevation via switchbacks before settling into a moderate climb along a west-facing slope. The trail climbs through dense forest at first as it approaches a trio of sharp but widely spaced switchbacks. From the first switchback, you catch your first glimpse west toward Little Baldy's big brother, Big

Baldy Ridge, as well as the rounded crowns of sequoias at Muir Grove.

Shortly after the last switchback at 1.1 miles (1.8 km), the trail evens out to pass through a recovering forest graced with dense thickets of young red firs that looks very much like a Christmas tree farm. This stretch of easy walking over mildly undulating terrain continues until 1.5 miles (2.5 km), where you reach the base of Little Baldy. A short scramble leads you out of tree cover and onto Little Baldy's rounded summit.

Once upon the summit, you can swivel your body around to take in the full extent of the view. The Silliman Crest

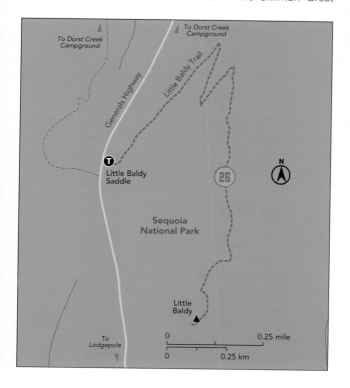

Silliman Crest viewed from Little Baldy's summit

culminating in Mount Silliman is the dominant landscape on the skyline to the northeast and east. Beyond Silliman Crest, you will be able to pick out upper Tokopah Valley, Alta Peak, and beyond toward the serrated ridgeline of the Great Western Divide. The rugged folds of Yucca Creek's drainage melt away toward the North Fork Kaweah River canyon while the obscuring haze of the San Joaquin Valley sets the sinking sun ablaze in fiery oranges, reds, and purples.

27 MUIR GROVE

Distance: 4.6 miles (7.4 km)
Elevation gain: 750 feet (230 m)
High point: 6869 feet (2094 m)
Difficulty: Moderate
Trail surface: Dirt
Map: USGS 7.5-min Muir Grove
GPS: 36.633920°, -118.817465°
Notes: Day use only; good for kids; restrooms located within Dorst Creek Campground

If you were to visit only Giant Forest and no other sequoia groves, you might think that all groves unfurl across broad, gently sloping plateaus yielding to impressive declivities. But the seventy-five groves sprinkled across the Sierra come in a wide variety of shapes and sizes, each of which is distinct from the next. Some groves line canyon bottoms along a water-course. Some groves cluster on steep, inaccessible hillsides on high canyon walls. One particularly memorable grove, Muir Grove, clusters along a knoll overlooking Dorst Creek.

GETTING THERE

Driving: From the Ash Mountain Entrance, follow Generals Highway north for 29.4 miles (47.1 km), passing the village of Lodgepole and the Little Baldy Trailhead. Turn left to enter Dorst Creek Campground (open mid-June through September) and drive to the west end of the campground to a day-use parking area south of the group campsites. From this parking area, walk north toward the group campsites, and turn left into the campsite loop. The Muir Grove Trailhead lies on the southwest corner of this loop. If the campground is closed, park along the highway just outside of the campground and walk through.

Transit: Purple Route 3 runs from Lodgepole to the entrance of Dorst Creek Campground. From there, walk west to the Muir Grove Trailhead.

ON THE TRAIL

The approach to Muir Grove begins with a gentle descent through mixed-conifer forest dominated by sugar pine and white fir. After dipping into a stream-lined ravine crowded with leafy dogwoods at 0.4 mile (0.6 km), the trail ascends a ridge dividing the first ravine from a second ravine farther east. Once the trail crests this ridge, views open up from a spacious granite outcrop. Looking east and north, you can trace the various tributaries of Dorst Creek as their drainages swell toward the forested Kings-Kaweah Divide and the Jennie Lakes Wilderness to the northeast.

After stopping to enjoy the views from the outcrop, descend toward a second stream-lined ravine at 1.7 miles (2.7 km), which is also crowded with dogwoods. Once past this ravine, the trail begins ascending once again as it climbs toward a saddle crowned with giant sequoias. The first sequoias appear before the saddle, but the most memorable trees are clustered in a circle directly upon the saddle itself.

Although a good part of the grove spills into a drainage and is thus difficult to access, the heart of Muir Grove is as memorable a forest scene as you will find. This nearly circular arrangement of giants surrounds an open clearing that evokes numerous possibilities within vivid imaginations. Could this have been an American Indian meeting place? Is

The heart of Muir Grove

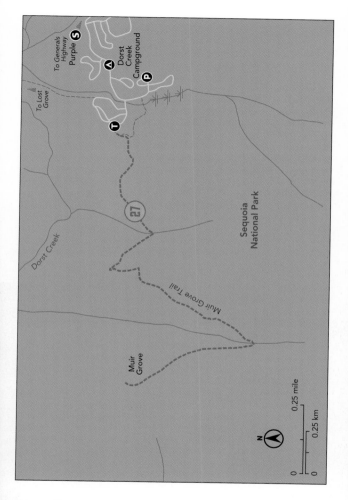

this an Entmoot that became frozen in time? Did John Muir once stand upon this spot and assume he had stumbled upon a pantheon of woodland gods? Whatever tone your musings take, Muir Grove is sure to leave a lasting impression.

REDWOOD CANYON

Redwood Canyon's sequoia groves—acknowledged as the world's largest—became a part of Kings Canyon National Park in 1940. This chapter describes two trips within Redwood Canyon that showcase the forest's vitality and the groves' impressive scales. Two additional trips follow trails along the northern and eastern rim of the canyon to Buena Vista Peak and Big Baldy Ridge, respectively. Although the two peaks stand outside the sequoia groves, their exposed granitic outcrops and outstanding position allow sweeping views ranging from the Monarch Divide to the north and the Great Western Divide to the south.

Backpackers can utilize a small number of campsites nestled into a grove of sequoias along the banks of Redwood Creek, the canyon's principal watercourse. Few places remain within the parks where hikers can camp beneath giant sequoias in a grove that has been left relatively untouched by human development. Visitation is strictly controlled by the park's permit and quota system, so apply for permits as early as possible.

28 BIG BALDY RIDGE

Distance: 6 miles (9.7 km)
Elevation gain: 1700 feet (520 m)
High point: 8209 feet (2502 m)

OPPOSITE: *The Big Baldy Ridge Trail meanders through a carpet of manzanita beneath the shade of red firs (Route 28).*

Difficulty: Challenging
Trail surface: Dirt with occasional rocky stretches
Map: USGS 7.5-min General Grant Grove
GPS: 36.697635°, -118.878863°
Notes: Day use only; minor routefinding; no restroom at trailhead

> The trail to Big Baldy follows an undulating ridgeline dotted with several granitic outcrops devoid of trees. These outcrops give the ridge the fanciful appearance of having lost significant patches of hair, thus spawning the ridge's name. Big Baldy Peak, a prominent high point standing about halfway along both the ridge and the route, is one possible destination. Hikers who aren't averse to a bit of routefinding on unmaintained trail can reach an even more spectacular bald spot above a promontory that drops precipitously to the North Fork Kaweah River to the south.

GETTING THERE

From Kings Canyon National Park's Big Stump Entrance, drive east on CA Highway 180 for 1.6 miles (2.6 km) to a Y intersection and turn right onto Generals Highway. Continue driving south for 6.6 miles (10.6 km) to the Big Baldy Ridge Trailhead.

ON THE TRAIL

Step onto the Big Baldy Trail and follow it south on a short incline through red fir forest. At 0.4 mile (0.6 km), the trail reaches the ridge's first bald spot, and here you will find colorful metamorphic rock that seems at odds with the usual salt-and-pepper Sierra granite. Your first glimpse of views across Redwood Canyon occur here as well, and this view will be your companion for the remainder of the hike.

The trail dips back into the trees until reemerging at the next bald spot at 1.1 miles (1.8 km). If you look southwest

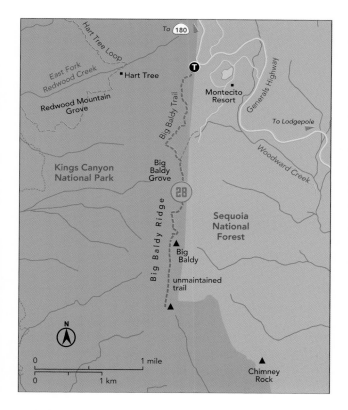

and downslope, you may be able to pick out some of the rounded sequoia crowns belonging to Big Baldy's name-sake sequoia grove. Following this second bald spot, the trail commences its most prolonged stretch of climbing as it gains 400 feet (120 m) over the next 0.6 mile (1 km) before reaching Big Baldy Peak.

If sticking to clear, established trails is your cup of tea, Big Baldy Peak is a good place to stop. You can enjoy stellar views from this perch, which include the Monarch Divide, the Great Western Divide, and the Silliman Crest. If you

The sudden drop-off at the south end of Big Baldy Ridge

turn around here, it's a 4.6-mile (7.4-km) hike with roughly 1000 feet (305 m) of elevation gain. With that said, the ridge gets more interesting as you go along, especially once you reach the final bald spot above a startling, view-packed promontory.

The trail heading south from Big Baldy Peak is no longer maintained, but the tread remains clear enough to follow without too much difficulty. The main challenge comes from downed trees, which may lie across the path and make it hard to locate the path on the other side of the tree. So long as you are patient about sniffing out the trail, you won't go astray.

You reach the final bald spot at just over 3 miles (4.8 km). Although this peak is a bit lower than Big Baldy Peak, the views are even better, especially those that look south into the North Fork Kaweah River canyon. Chimney Rock, a crag that looks like a chimney, rises from dense forest about 1 crow-flying mile (1.6 km) to the southeast. The soaring high country of Sequoia and Kings Canyon National Parks also remains visible, rounding out the panorama with a dash of grandeur.

29 BUENA VISTA PEAK

Distance: 2 miles (3.2 km)
Elevation gain: 450 feet (140 m)
High point: 7605 feet (2318 m)
Difficulty: Easy
Trail surface: Dirt with one large granite outcrop
Map: USGS 7.5-min General Grant Grove
GPS: 36.718261°, -118.896962°
Notes: Day use only; good for kids; no restroom at the trailhead

Not all mountaintops in Kings Canyon National Park fall into the domain of masochistic hikers with nuclear-powered quadriceps and calves of steel. For novices, children, or simply those looking for a casual hike with great views, Buena Vista Peak is a perfect mountaintop from which to enjoy a picnic lunch or to observe the sun setting into the San Joaquin Valley.

GETTING THERE

From Kings Canyon National Park's Big Stump Entrance, drive east on CA Highway 180 for 1.6 miles (2.6 km) to a Y intersection and turn right onto Generals Highway. Continue driving south for 4.7 miles (7.6 km) to the Buena Vista Peak Trailhead.

Admiring the view toward Kings Canyon from Buena Vista Peak

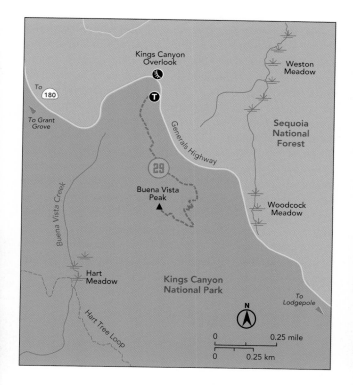

ON THE TRAIL

This easy 2-mile (3.2-km) out-and-back route climbs obliquely along the east face of Buena Vista Peak through scenic rock outcrops and a tranquil forest of sugar pines and white firs. Routefinding is simple as the trail heads southwest and uphill until reaching a switchback at 0.8 mile that presents an unexpected challenge. This turn is easy to miss on the return journey, especially if you're descending after sunset. Be sure to take a good look at the area surrounding the junction so that you recognize it on your way back.

After this switchback, follow the trail west through scattered Jeffrey pines toward the summit. If you don't mind looking a little silly, stick your nose into the grooves of a Jeffrey pine's bark and inhale deeply. The overwhelming scent of butterscotch and vanilla is sure to please your senses and compensate for a bit of teasing from your hiking companions.

You soon reach the boulder-studded summit overlooking the depths of Redwood Canyon to the west, the Monarch Divide to the north, and the Great Western Divide to the southeast. During summer, the sun sinks over Redwood Mountain, setting the smoggy Central Valley sky ablaze with rich, fiery colors. This is a great place to relax with friends, perhaps enjoying an afternoon picnic or even an evening sack dinner capped off with a memorable sunset.

One word of warning: if you bring your kids, keep a close eye on them near the summit. There's a sheer cliff on the peak's west face that may cause some parental anxiety.

30 SUGARBOWL LOOP

Distance: 6.9 miles (11.1 km)
Elevation gain: 1400 feet (430 m)
High point: 6954 feet (2120 m)
Difficulty: Challenging
Trail surface: Dirt
Map: USGS 7.5-min General Grant Grove
GPS: 36.708078°, -118.921037°
Notes: Suitable for backpacking; no food storage lockers at campsites; restrooms at trailhead

A passage through the Sugarbowl Loop on an early morning in spring reveals sunlight filtering down through the boughs of towering sequoia trees. Deer browse half-seen in dense thickets of dogwood while snow plants rise from duff on the forest floor like crimson aliens. This otherworldly, looping route visits the "grove within a grove" at the Sugarbowl, a pristine stand of sequoia trees nestled into a nook on the flanks of Redwood Mountain.

GETTING THERE

From Kings Canyon National Park's Big Stump Entrance, drive east on CA Highway 180 for 1.6 miles (2.6 km) to a Y intersection, and turn right onto Generals Highway. Continue south on Generals Highway for 3.6 miles (5.8 km) to the signed Redwood Canyon Access Road. Continue on the unpaved road for 1.9 miles (3.1 km) to the parking area at Redwood Saddle. Note that this road may close when it is snowbound during the winter and spring.

ON THE TRAIL

From the signed Sugarbowl Trailhead, proceed due south to ascend the south-trending ridge of Redwood Mountain. The steep climb gradually settles into a gentler grade as the trail meanders between the east and west side of the ridge. As you progress, observe the profound effects of slope aspect. The drier west slopes receive more direct sun exposure, and the high rate of evaporation suits hardy Jeffrey pines and black oaks. The east slope holds moisture much longer, supporting sequoias and firs. The distance between these two distinct biomes is often little more than a few meters. In addition to the intriguing vacillations between dramatically different biomes, you will enjoy an ever-improving view east toward Big Baldy Ridge as you climb.

After reaching the route's high point at 2 miles (3.2 km), the trail descends for 0.5 mile (0.8 km) into the Sugarbowl. This nearly pure stand of sequoias presents a captivating stopping point before you descend into Redwood Canyon. Most of the sequoias here are average-sized, but the grove is noteworthy for being nearly all sequoias. Most sequoias

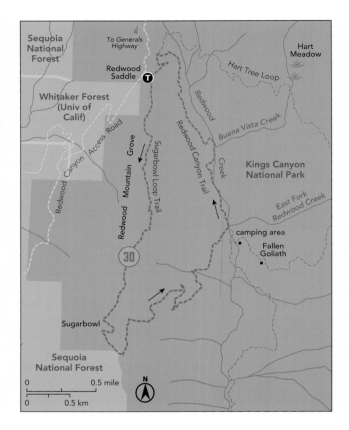

grow alongside other trees, mainly white fir and sugar pines, and pure groves are rare. Furthermore, the grove's sheltered nature offers a secluded niche from which to enjoy a bit of solitude.

From the Sugarbowl, the trail crosses over a low-saddle and begins a zig-zagging descent into Redwood Canyon. About halfway through the descent, the trail passes through a dense thicket of young sequoias. These saplings are the beneficiaries of the park's prescribed burn program, which mimics the role of natural wildfires in maintaining and promoting the health of sequoia groves.

At 4.8 miles (7.7 km), the trail reaches the bottom of Redwood Canyon at a three-way junction with the Redwood Canyon Trail. If you're backpacking, turn right and walk down canyon about 100 yards (90 m) to a spot where downed sequoias allow you to cross the creek. The designated camping area lies on the opposite bank of Redwood Creek beneath several large sequoias. If day hiking, make a left at the junction and begin a gentle ascent north along Redwood Creek.

The remaining 2 miles (3.2 km) north along the bottom of Redwood Canyon pass through dense thickets of dogwoods proliferating along the banks of the creek. In spring, the dogwoods are laden with thousands of showy white blossoms. In autumn, the tree's leaves turn a vivid red, adding an unexpected splash of fall color to the route. Numerous sequoias ranging from small to above-average size tower above while

A summer thunderstorm and Big Baldy Ridge seen from the Sugarbowl Loop

Redwood Creek trickles along, often unseen due to a thick jungle of willows. At 6.6 miles (10.6 km), the trail merges with the Hart Tree Loop and winds uphill, generally south, back to the parking area to close the loop at 6.9 miles (11.1 km).

31 HART TREE LOOP

Distance: 7.6 miles (12.2 km)
Elevation gain: 1500 feet (460 m)
High point: 6417 feet (1956 m)
Difficulty: Challenging
Trail surface: Dirt
Map: USGS 7.5-min General Grant Grove
GPS: 36.708078°, -118.921037°
Notes: Suitable for backpacking; no food storage lockers at campsites; restroom at the trailhead

> Although the sequoia groves in Redwood Canyon mostly contain trees in a greater density than other equivalent groves, there are only a handful of specimens that stand out as notably large. Discovered in 1880 by a man named Michael Hart, the Hart Tree is recognized as the twenty-first largest sequoia in the world, although at one time, prior to accurate measurements, it was considered to be fourth largest. Along the way, hikers will enjoy stops at a meadow, a small waterfall, and a lush corridor of riparian trees along Redwood Creek.

GETTING THERE

From Kings Canyon National Park's Big Stump Entrance, drive east on CA Highway 180 for 1.6 miles (2.6 km) to a Y intersection, and turn right onto Generals Highway. Continue south on Generals Highway for 3.6 miles (5.8 km) to the signed Redwood Canyon Access Road. Continue on the unpaved road for 1.9 miles (3.1 km) to the parking area at

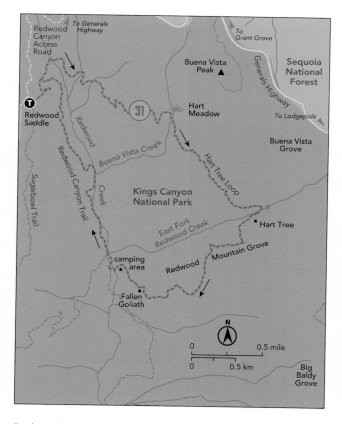

Redwood Saddle. Note that this road may close when it is snowbound during the winter and spring.

ON THE TRAIL

Starting out, follow the Redwood Canyon Trail heading northeast, away from Redwood Saddle, to a junction with the Hart Tree Loop (your return point) at 0.4 mile (0.6 km). From here, turn left onto the Heart Tree Loop, passing a handful of logged stumps, the legacy of a limited logging operation that fortunately did not touch the remainder of the grove. The trail next wends in and out of several tributary ravines with a short stop at a burnt-out log that some creative soul transformed into a cabin. The cabin doesn't look as cozy as Hale Tharp's (see Route 18), but it's still a fun curiosity to explore.

Redwood Creek's cool, soothing waters

Just before reaching Hart Meadow at 2.2 miles (3.5 km), you emerge from the forest at a granite outcrop to survey the canyon from an open, sunny spot. Just beyond here, the trail skirts Hart Meadow before crossing its feeder creek, Buena Vista Creek. After passing over a modest ridge, the trail then begins the descent toward Redwood Creek. At just shy of the halfway point (3.4 miles/5.5 km), consider a short break at a spot where East Fork Redwood Creek spills over a 15-foot (5-m) ledge surrounded by mosses and ferns. This waterfall can dry up later in the season, and its flow is at its best during May and June.

Just beyond the waterfall, a short connector trail at 3.4 miles (5.5 km) leads sharply uphill to the base of the Hart Tree. Note the massive burn scar on the upslope side of the tree; many sequoias feature burn scars on their upslope sides due to logs tumbling downhill and coming to rest at the base of the tree. When a fire rolls through, the log smolders for an extended period, leaving a significant but harmless scar on the sequoia's flank. Nearly all old sequoias have some kind of burn scar, but after a period of time the bark will regrow over the scar, eventually hiding it from view.

An extended descent leading to Redwood Creek awaits after the Hart Tree. Near the bottom of the descent, you will pass by the Fallen Goliath, a massive fallen sequoia, before the trail bottoms out along the bank of Redwood Creek. Nearby camping spots offer a resting spot for backpackers. A pair of logs about 50 yards (45 m) apart allow you to cross the creek and reach the Redwood Canyon Trail.

To complete the loop, turn right to follow the Redwood Canyon Trail through the lush corridor of dogwoods uphill and back to Redwood Saddle.

GRANT GROVE

The sequoias in the Grant Grove region, including Big Stump Grove, North Grove, and Grant Grove itself, were among some of the first to be seen, admired, coveted, and ultimately protected by the federal government. American Indians had already known of the region for years, but the first European American visitors to the area encountered the General Grant Tree around the beginning of the Civil War. Stories about the immensity of the vegetation met with disbelief from Americans in the East, who could scarcely believe that anything could grow so large given how relatively modest the vegetation tends to be east of the Mississippi River.

Most recreation in Grant Grove centers around the village and the General Grant Tree. While the tree itself is a sight not to be missed, Grant Grove also features impressive views from Park Ridge, secluded waterfalls trickling through thickets of azalea bushes beneath tranquil forests along the Sunset Trail, and an informative stroll through a logged grove that is recovering at impressive rates in the Big Stump Basin.

Grant Grove Village features a market, restaurants, the Kings Canyon Visitor Center, the John Muir Lodge, two standard campgrounds (Azalea and Sunset), and one campground featuring individual and medium-sized group sites (Crystal Springs Campground). This profusion of visitor services can make Grant Grove feel a little hectic, but like all destinations in the Sequoia–Kings Canyon frontcountry, walk

OPPOSITE: *Shafts of morning light filter down to the Grant Grove Trail (Route 34).*

a ways on a quiet forest trail, and you will quickly leave the hustle and bustle behind.

32 BIG STUMP GROVE

Distance: 1.3 miles (2.1 km)
Elevation gain: 250 feet (75 m)
High point: 6371 feet (1942 m)
Difficulty: Easy
Trail surface: Dirt
Map: USGS 7.5-min General Grant Grove
GPS: 36.720944°, -118.970797°
Notes: Day use only; good for children; restroom at trailhead

> Visitors who view only the General Grant Tree in its well-protected environs might walk away with the impression that human beings have always been on their best behavior around sequoia groves. Big Stump Grove disabuses visitors of that assumption, but it also offers valuable lessons on history and sequoia ecology. The numerous "big stumps" are the legacy of several decades of rampant timber exploitation that occurred throughout the groves in the Kings River drainage, and the rapid recovery of the grove combined with a pair of lush meadows provides a welcome counterpoint.

GETTING THERE

From Kings Canyon National Park's Big Stump Entrance, drive north on CA Highway 180 for 0.7 mile (1.3 km), and turn left into the signed Big Stump Picnic Area. Find the Big Stump Trailhead just left of the restrooms.

ON THE TRAIL

From the Big Stump picnic area, follow the Big Stump Trail southeast and downhill through mixed-conifer forest of

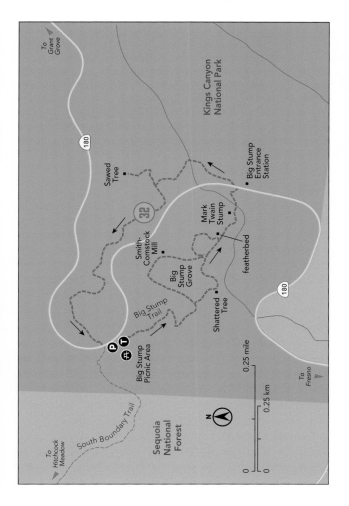

adolescent sequoias, sugar pine, white fir, and Jeffrey pine. Younger sequoias tend to appear more like other conifers when they are young. They grow upward at a rapid pace, and they only begin to grow outward once they've reached their full height. Mixed into these adolescent sequoias, you will find several stumps of the grove's original monarchs rising out of a bed of ferns.

At 0.3 mile (0.5 km), the trail splits where it reaches a large, sunny meadow; both branches merge on the opposite side of the meadow. The right fork leads toward Shattered Tree, a large sequoia that shattered upon impact after it was cut down. Shattered Tree demonstrates how brittle sequoias are and how poor their timber was for any uses other than creating items such as shingles, fence posts, toothpicks, and grapevine stakes. The left branch of the trail loops around the meadow and passes the site of the Smith-Comstock Mill at 0.4 mile (0.6 km). The two branches of the trail reunite at 0.5 mile (0.8 km) near a sign indicating the presence of a nearby "featherbed." Loggers would dig trenches and fill them with branches and other soft vegetation in an attempt to cushion the impact of a falling sequoia. Without such cushioning, the resulting impact would shatter the tree.

Beyond the featherbed junction, continue eastbound toward a second, smaller meadow. The Mark Twain Stump lies on the eastern end of this meadow. The stump's tree was the only one in the grove not cut down for timber. Cross sections of the tree were sent to New York and London to demonstrate the size of the sequoia. The wide, spacious stump has a staircase leading to the top, which gives you a nice perspective on how wide sequoia bases can be.

The trail continues beyond the Mark Twain Stump, crossing under CA Highway 180 at 0.7 mile (1.1 km). Once on the other side of the highway, the trail arcs back toward Big Stump picnic area. One final diversion at 0.8 mile (1.3 km) leads to the Sawed Tree. Here, a particularly rebellious sequoia proved so difficult to cut down that the loggers called it quits and left it alone (good on you, Sawed Tree!). Continue past the Sawed Tree and cross under CA 180 to return to Big Stump Picnic Area at 1.3 miles (2.1 km).

The Shattered Tree demonstrates the futility of sequoia logging.

GOING FARTHER

For an optional side trip, consider following the South Boundary Trail northwest for 0.7 mile (1.1 km) from the parking area to Hitchcock Meadow. A tributary to Sequoia Creek feeds this meadow, creating a lush blanket of vegetation rimmed by adolescent sequoias and fragrant azaleas.

33 SUNSET LOOP

Distance: 6.3 miles (10.1 km)
Elevation gain: 1200 feet (370 m)
High point: 6572 feet (2003 m)
Difficulty: Challenging
Trail surface: Dirt
Map: USGS 7.5-min General Grant Grove
GPS: 36.747022°, -118.973200°
Notes: Day use only; restroom at trailhead

> Waterfalls, sequoia groves, meadows, streams, fragrant thickets of azalea, and a generous measure of solitude are the principal attractions on this half-day loop through several quiet corners of the Grant Grove area. Although Grant Grove is not famous for its waterfalls, this route leads you to two spots where you can enjoy the musical sounds of Sequoia Creek as it spills over a pair of falls in a peaceful, wooded canyon.

GETTING THERE

From Kings Canyon National Park's Big Stump Entrance, drive east for 1.7 miles (2.7 km) toward a junction with Generals Highway, and turn left to continue heading north on CA Highway 180. After 3.3 miles (5.3 km), turn left onto a road indicating the General Grant Tree. After 0.8 mile (1.3 km), arrive at the General Grant parking lot. The signed trailhead for Grant Grove Village Trail is on the east side of the parking lot.

ON THE TRAIL

First, find the trail leading east from the Grant Grove parking area past the fallen Michigan Tree. Note that this trail is separate from the Grant Grove loop, so if you find yourself on a paved trail leading toward the General Grant Tree, you have gone the wrong way. Once you locate the Grant Grove Village Trail, follow it east and then south through Azalea and Sunset Campgrounds. The frequent road crossings and somewhat disjointed trail tread require attention to ensure that you don't go astray, but clear signage helps you remain on course.

Ella Falls's multi-tiered cascade

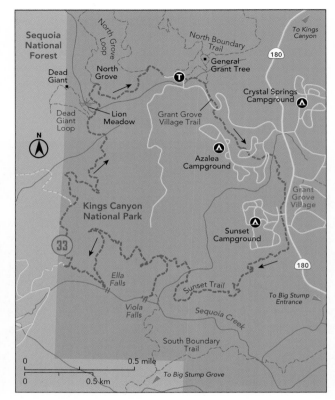

Continue past Sunset Campground via a trail paralleling CA 180 past the unseen but heard hubbub of Grant Grove Village. After turning right onto the Sunset Trail at 1.2 miles (1.9 km), follow the trail as it weaves through heavily wooded ravines before flattening out at a lush basin fed by a tributary to Sequoia Creek, and Sequoia Creek itself at 2.2 miles (3.5 km). This area features copious growths of Western azalea, a deciduous shrub whose showy white blossoms emit an intoxicating perfume. At the junction with the South Boundary Trail (2.4 miles/3.9 km), turn left to visit Viola

Falls. Although modest in size, Viola Falls's melodious tones hint at a possible reason for its name, and the cool shade of sequoias makes this an alluring stopping point.

After your visit to Viola Falls, return to the Sunset Trail and continue descending through dense forest recovering from a recent fire. At a sharp switchback near the banks of Sequoia Creek (3.9 miles/6.3 km), look to your left to find Ella Falls, a multitiered cascade 50 yards (45 m) from the trail. Thick brush and boulders make it difficult to reach the base of the falls, but they are best enjoyed from afar anyway.

After the falls comes the hard part. Follow a connector path north to avoid continuing along a dirt road to Sequoia Lake YMCA Camp (4.25 miles/6.8 km), and begin climbing on a winding dirt road uphill through recovering forest before eventually reaching Lion Meadow and North Grove at 5.4 miles (8.7 km) and 5.9 miles (9.5 km), respectively. This uphill-at-the-end feature of the trail will require effort at a time when you may be ready for cruise control, but such is the price you pay for experiencing the quiet side of Grant Grove. At 6.3 miles (10.1 km), the dirt road reaches a gated overflow parking area for Grant Grove. Continue through the parking area to return to your car.

34 GRANT GROVE

Distance: 0.5 mile (0.8 km)
Elevation gain: 150 feet (45 m)
High point: 6411 feet (1954 m)
Difficulty: Easy
Trail surface: Paved
Map: USGS 7.5-min General Grant Grove
GPS: 36.747022°, -118.973200°
Notes: Day use only; good for kids; ADA accessible; restroom at trailhead

The Grant Grove area's namesake sequoia grove features some of the largest and best examples of massive sequoias anywhere outside of Giant Forest in Sequoia National Park. The grove's monarch, the General Grant Tree, is second only to the General Sherman Tree in size. Numerous other impressive trees and historic features within the grove pack this short hike with a wealth of highlights.

GETTING THERE

From Kings Canyon National Park's Big Stump Entrance, drive east for 1.7 miles (2.7 km) toward a junction with Generals Highway, and turn left to continue heading north on CA Highway 180. After 3.3 miles (5.3 km), turn left onto a road indicating the General Grant Tree. After 0.8 mile (1.3 km), arrive at the General Grant parking lot. Your starting point is the signed trailhead for Grant Grove Trail, which lies on the north side of the parking lot.

ON THE TRAIL

From the signed trailhead, head north on the paved path and immediately encounter a T junction for the two branches of the paved, accessible Grant Grove Trail. Going left or right will bring you back to the start after a half mile of easy hiking, but for the sake of following the landmarks described here, turn left. A gentle switchback brings you past a massive sequoia and several impressive specimens of sugar pine before arriving at the Fallen Monarch.

The hollowed-out Fallen Monarch has experienced multiple uses over the years. In the early days of park history, visitors used the hollow log as both a shelter and a saloon. Today, this curiosity doubles both as a desirable climbing object for children and a cut-off that leads to the second half of the Grant Grove Loop.

Continuing beyond the Fallen Monarch, you'll pass numerous impressive sequoias, some named, before arriving at

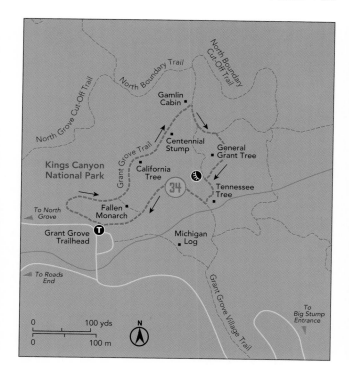

the Centennial Stump. The tree that once stood here was chopped down, cut into pieces, shipped across the country to Philadelphia, and reassembled for the Centennial International Exhibition. Viewers thought the tree a joke due to its preposterous proportions and dubbed it "the California Hoax." On any given Sunday over a century ago, teachers conducted Sunday school classes atop the massive stump.

After Centennial Stump, you reach Gamlin Cabin and a junction leading away to the North Boundary Trail. Originally constructed by cattle ranchers, the cabin later became the headquarters for the tiny General Grant National Park upon the park's inception in 1890.

The Tennessee Tree is one of many notable sequoias in Grant Grove.

The trail makes a pronounced right turn as it continues toward the General Grant Tree. A mini loop encircles the 267-foot-tall tree (81 m), reaching a point where you can observe the massive burn scar on the north side of the trunk. Since the tree is surrounded by other significant sequoias and towering sugar pines, it can be hard to get a full appreciation for just how big it is. Continue downhill toward a viewpoint that allows you to view the entire tree.

After the Grant Tree, you reach the final highlight on the route: the Tennessee Tree. Fires burned out a large chunk of the tree's base, leaving it to stand on a relatively thin strip of wood. From the Tennessee Tree, the trail leads downhill back to the parking area.

35 PARK RIDGE

Distance: 5.6 miles (9 km)
Elevation gain: 1000 feet (300 m)
High point: 7772 feet (2369 m)
Difficulty: Challenging
Trail surface: Dirt
Map: USGS 7.5-min General Grant Grove
GPS: 36.753830°, -118.946528°
Notes: Day use only; trail is ADA accessible up to Panoramic Point; restrooms at trailhead

The best views as well as some of the most enjoyable hiking in Grant Grove can be found along a narrow figure-eight route that follows the undulations of Park Ridge from Panoramic Point to the Park Ridge Fire Lookout Tower. At various points, you will enjoy unparalleled views to the north, south, east, and west, with the eastern views over the Kings Canyon high country among some of the most impressive vistas in the park's frontcountry.

GETTING THERE

From Kings Canyon National Park's Big Stump Entrance, drive east for 1.7 miles (2.7 km) toward a junction with Generals Highway, and turn left to continue heading north on CA Highway 180. After 3.3 miles (5.3 km), turn right onto an unnamed road signed for Crystal Springs Campground and Panoramic Point. Drive for 2.4 miles (3.9 km) on the narrow, winding road, passing Crystal Springs Campground and the

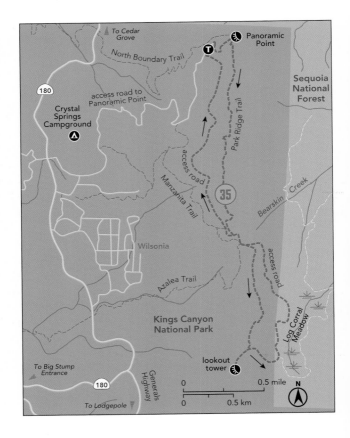

John Muir Lodge, until the roads end at the Panoramic Point Trailhead.

ON THE TRAIL

From the signed trailhead for Panoramic Point, follow the paved, accessible trail from the parking area as it switchbacks uphill to Panoramic Point. The views from Panoramic Point are outstanding, and they take in both the Hume Lake area as well as the serrated ridge of the Monarch Divide. If you crave only a short exploration and some great views, Panoramic Point delivers on both counts. You can turn back here for a 0.4-mile (0.6-km) hike with 60 feet (20 m) of elevation gain.

However, the views only improve, and the hiking only gets better if you continue on the Park Ridge Trail. Find the beginning of the trail from the south end of the Panoramic Trail viewing area. The first quarter of the trail undulates over several exposed high points, which punctuate a pleasant forest of red fir and sugar pine. About halfway along the ridge at 1.6 miles (2.6 km), the Park Ridge Trail reaches a six-way junction with the unpaved access road to the lookout (your return route), the Manzanita Trail, and the Azalea Trail. The continuation of the trail crosses over the road at this junction to run just west of the access road.

The trail, now traversing the west slope of the ridge, surveys views west over Grant Grove and beyond toward Squaw Valley and Fresno. After several more undulations over the ridge's rolling topography, the trail dead ends at the access road to the lookout at 2.8 miles (4.5 km). Turn right to take a short stroll along the road toward a handful of outbuildings and the metal lookout tower itself. You can climb up the stairs unless ice and snow make them dangerous or the tower is closed to nonpark personnel. From the tower, you can scan the horizon to see the rolling foothills that swell toward Grant Grove. Sequoia-studded Redwood Mountain

Park Ridge is one of the best sunrise hikes in Kings Canyon National Park.

looms to the southwest, and the higher country surrounding Big Meadows swells to the southeast. As before, the most impressive views are those north toward the Monarch Divide and beyond to Kings Canyon's high country.

The return route can follow the same trail you came in on, but a loop back on the access road has a few attractions of its own. First and foremost, the road does not undulate nearly as much as the single-track trail, so you will spare yourself a fair amount of up and down on the return journey. You will pass spring-fed Log Corral Meadow (3.4 miles/5.5 km) after dipping briefly into Sequoia National Forest on the east side of the ridge. After crossing the west side of the ridge beyond the six-way junction (4.1 miles/6.6 km), the road passes through open, sunny hillsides blanketed with manzanita and chock-full of wide-ranging views. Finally, the road reenters dense fir forest surrounding another lush meadow before terminating at the main road just west of the trailhead. Turn right here to return to the parking area.

KINGS CANYON

Imagine a cool spring morning the day after the long drive into Kings Canyon. You have commenced your own exploration in order to compare notes with John Muir, who claimed that Kings Canyon rivaled the iconic depths of Yosemite Valley. You step onto the flat trail, shaded by ponderosa pine and incense cedars. A scruffy understory of manzanita thrives in open, sunny pockets, within which you get your first looks down canyon toward the confluence of Bubbs Creek and the South Fork. Granite walls soar thousands of feet above the canyon, rising vertically from the mighty South Fork Kings River. Some fifty yards off the trail, a black bear follows his nose to enticing morsels on the forest floor, while the distant roar of the river, now swollen from a melting snowpack, offers the promise of a powerful spectacle of raging water in your near future.

Such are the pleasures of Kings Canyon, one of the deepest and most impressive canyons in the United States. Thanks to the canyon's remoteness, and perhaps unfair and irrelevant comparisons to Yosemite Valley, Kings Canyon maintains a somewhat quieter and more tranquil ambiance than other hubs of activity in the southern Sierra. While the canyon's four campgrounds and single lodge often fill up during the summer, it is not uncommon to walk for hours along the canyon floor without encountering other hikers.

Services within the canyon include the aforementioned campgrounds: Sheep Creek, Sentinel, Canyon View Group

OPPOSITE: *Kings Canyon's signature formation, the Sentinel, stands watch over Zumwalt Meadow (Route 38).*

Campground, and Moraine Campground. In addition to camping, Cedar Grove Lodge provides more refined sleeping arrangements as well as a café, store, market, laundromat, showers, ranger station, and amphitheater for ranger programs. Roads End in the heart of the canyon issues backcountry permits while serving as one of the principal and most popular entry points into the backcountry. Several routes leave Roads End to penetrate the backcountry from the Woods Creek, Bubbs Creek, and Copper Creek Trailheads.

36 DON CECIL TRAIL TO SHEEP CREEK FALLS

Distance: 1.8 miles (2.9 km)
Elevation gain: 600 feet (180 m)
High point: 5190 feet (1582 m)
Difficulty: Moderate
Trail surface: Dirt
Map: USGS 7.5-min Cedar Grove
GPS: 36.790018°, -118.671097°
Notes: Day use only; good for kids; restroom adjacent to trailhead near Sentinel Campground

Up until the opening of the road into Cedar Grove, the Don Cecil sheep trail was the primary way in or out of Kings Canyon. The lower reaches of the Kings River proved too rugged for foot travel, and the river's thundering cascades made it impassable by boat. Today's Don Cecil Trail remains relatively faithful to the original track. A short section of the trail leads to Sheep Creek Falls, a lovely cascade spilling over granite slabs in a shaded grotto.

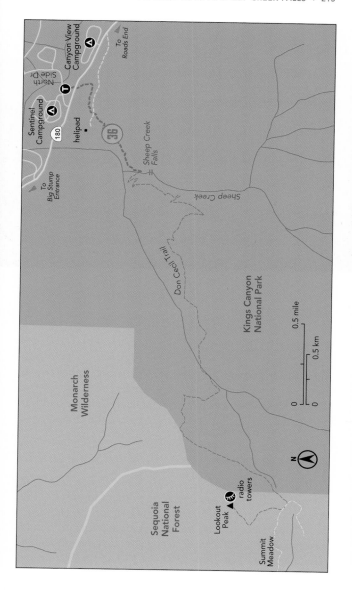

Surveying the entirety of Kings Canyon from Lookout Peak

GETTING THERE

From Kings Canyon National Park's Big Stump Entrance, drive east for 1.7 miles (2.7 km) on CA Highway 180, and keep left at a junction with Generals Highway. Continue driving east for another 31 miles (49.9 km) into Cedar Grove. Turn left onto North Side Drive leading to Cedar Grove Lodge. Make the next left into Sentinel Campground and park in the day-use lot on the right before the campground entrance.

ON THE TRAIL

From the day-use parking area near the entrance to Sentinel Campground, follow a connector trail south toward CA 180, and cross the road to find the trailhead for the Don Cecil Trail. The trail begins an immediate steady ascent through mixed-conifer forest of incense cedar, sugar pine, ponderosa pine, and black oak. After 0.3 mile (0.5 km), cross the dirt road that leads to a helipad, and continue climbing. Occasional gaps in the forest cover reveal views down canyon toward imposing granite cliffs.

At 0.9 mile (1.5 km) and 500 feet (150 m) of climbing, the trail arrives at a wooden bridge spanning Sheep Creek. Above and below the bridge, the creek spills over granite slabs or trickles into small pools bedecked by ferns and shaded by oaks and alders. This charming spot makes a good turnaround point if you desire only an easy hike and a pretty waterfall. Be aware that Sheep Creek provides the water supply for Cedar Grove, so be sure not to do anything to contribute any special additives to the drinking water.

GOING FARTHER

Hikers with a masochistic bent and an appetite for views with a capital V can continue along the Don Cecil Trail as it grinds its way to spectacular views at Lookout Peak. At 5.1 miles (8.2 km) and 3600 feet (1100 m) of climbing, the trail crosses the Sequoia National Forest border, at which point you follow an informal 0.4-mile (0.6-km) path north toward the rocky summit of Lookout Peak. The roundtrip hike runs you 10.8 miles (17.3 km) with 3800 feet (1160 m) of elevation gain.

37 ROARING RIVER FALLS

Distance: 3.4 miles (5.5 km)
Elevation gain: 400 feet (120 m)
High point: 5023 feet (1531 m)
Difficulty: Moderate
Trail surface: Dirt
Map: USGS 7.5-min The Sphinx
GPS: 36.793684°, -118.598434°
Notes: Day use only; good for kids; restroom at trailhead

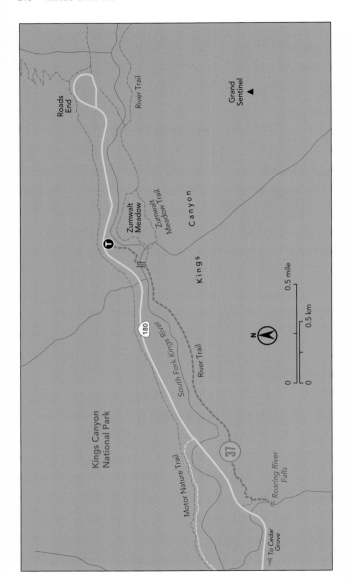

From its headwaters along the Kings-Kaweah Divide, the Roaring River collects enough snowmelt to earn the title of river despite serving as a tributary to the South Fork Kings River. True to its name, this river creates a mighty din as it plummets into a sculpted "punchbowl" framed with ponderosa pines and cedars. During times of peak run-off—usually late April through May—the deafening roar and prodigious mist kicked up by the falls produce a memorable sight.

GETTING THERE

From Kings Canyon National Park's Big Stump Entrance, drive east for 1.7 miles (2.7 km) on CA Highway 180, and keep left at a junction with Generals Highway. Continue driving east for another 31 miles (49.9 km) into Cedar Grove. Continue beyond Cedar Grove for another 4.5 miles (7.2 km) to the Zumwalt Meadow Trailhead.

ON THE TRAIL

Although you can reach Roaring River Falls by way of a short asphalt path leading south from CA 180 (3 miles/4.8 km east of Cedar Grove), this longer and more satisfying route follows the River Trail west from the shared trailhead accessing Zumwalt Meadow. At numerous spots, the trail follows close to the river, providing glimpses of the various moods of the South Fork Kings River along with excellent views across the canyon toward North Mountain, North Dome, Buck Peak, and the Grand Sentinel.

Follow the access trail connecting the Zumwalt Meadow Trailhead with the west-east trending River Trail as it passes through an open forest of ponderosa pine, black oak, and incense cedar. The South Fork Kings River meanders in a leisurely fashion to your left as you approach a steel suspension bridge spanning the river at 0.25 mile (0.4 km). West of the bridge, the river picks up speed as it flows over rapids, but the view east reveals the river at its most placid. When the river's

Roaring River Falls continues to roar well into the summer.

volume is low, a small beach on the east side of the bridge attracts swimmers. Use good judgment when entering the river. Even if it seems gentle, the current is strong all year long.

Beyond the bridge, the trail reaches a T junction with the left turn leading to Zumwalt Meadow and the right turn leading to Roaring River Falls. Turn right to head west, and follow the trail along the river over a gently descending course for the next 2 miles (3.2 km). Part of this forest continues to recover from a 2010 wildfire. Dense thickets of fire-following ferns and ceanothus thrive under the partial shade of this forest, and the trail occasionally has a wild, overgrown feel to it. At several spots, the trail edges along the river, although there aren't many good beaches from which to access the water.

After a wide arc where the trail approaches but does not quite touch CA 180 (1.4 miles/2.3 km), the trail bends back to the south to a junction with the paved trail leading to Roaring River Falls at 1.7 miles (2.7 km). Massive boulders and ponderosa pines frame the scene as the river spills into a deep, crystalline pool, creating a deafening roar that reverberates off the surrounding granite.

38   ZUMWALT MEADOW

Distance: 1.7 miles (2.7 km)
Elevation gain: 150 feet (45 m)
High point: 5051 feet (1540 m)
Difficulty: Easy
Trail surface: Dirt, with a section of wooden boardwalk
Map: USGS 7.5-min The Sphinx
GPS: 36.793684°, -118.598434°
Notes: Day use only; good for kids; restroom at trailhead

Kings Canyon's largest and most beautiful meadow lies alongside a sharp curve in the Kings River just west of Roads End. This kink in the riverbed temporarily slows the river, allowing some of its moisture to permeate a large, flat shelf rimmed by pines and carpeted in lush meadow vegetation. A short loop encircles Zumwalt Meadow, allowing access to countless beautiful montane scenes. Visit during the morning or afternoon to spot mule deer and black bears browsing the meadow.

GETTING THERE

From Kings Canyon National Park's Big Stump Entrance, drive east for 1.7 miles (2.7 km) on CA Highway 180, and keep left at a junction with Generals Highway. Continue driving east for another 31 miles (49.9 km) into Cedar Grove.

Zumwalt Meadow's lush splendor is set against Kings Canyon's austere granite.

Continue beyond Cedar Grove for another 4.5 miles (7.2 km) to the Zumwalt Meadow Trailhead.

ON THE TRAIL

The hike begins with a gentle stroll along the banks of the Kings River through a mixed forest of pine, oak, and cedar. Through the spaces in the forest, towering cliffs rise up, their sculpted faces awash in brilliant Sierran sunshine. The gentle music of the river resonates on your left as the formerly raucous symphony of the Kings eases into a bubbling adagio.

At 0.25 mile (0.4 km), cross a steel suspension bridge over the river. The bridge spans a point before the landscape recedes at a sharper angle, causing the water to pick up speed. Look west, and the river rumbles. Look east, and the placid Kings meanders lazily through a corridor of pine and cedar with the distant crags of Buck Peak looming to the east. A small beach just beyond the bridge becomes a

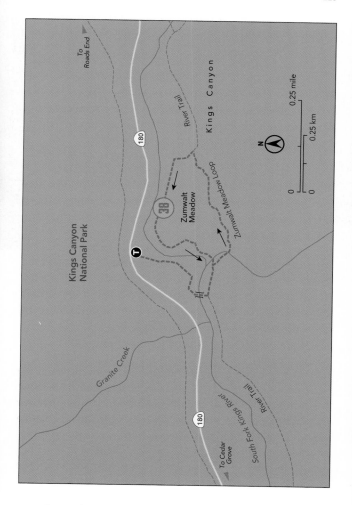

popular wading spot for families on hot summer days when the river's flow has diminished from lack of snowmelt.

On the south side of the bridge, turn left on the River Trail toward Zumwalt Meadow. Continue east to a second junction indicating the split for the Zumwalt Meadow Loop at 0.4 mile (0.6 km). Turn right to cross a large talus field bounding the southern edge of the meadow. The talus is composed primarily of boulders that have tumbled down from the cliffs above over the ages, leaving a rocky obstacle course that the trail climbs up and over. The elevated perspective also allows some good views across the meadow, which may be emerald green or gold depending on the season.

Once over the talus field, the trail curves to the left to meet the other half of the Zumwalt Meadow Loop in a clearing at 0.8 mile (1.3 km). The river trail continues straight here but keep left to continue the loop. A handful of house-sized granite boulders set in clearings may invite a bit of scrambling, and the opening in the tree cover allows views toward the towering pinnacle of Grand Sentinel to the southeast. After the trail passes through the clearing, it returns to the forest of ponderosa pine and incense cedar rising from a dense blanket of bracken fern on the forest floor. Several spots on the trail bring you right to the edge of the river, which flows along swiftly on your right.

The trail curves to the south along the northwest side of the meadow before reaching a wooden boardwalk (1.2 miles/1.9 km) that spans the western edge of the meadow where it abuts the river. A wooden observation deck looks east across the canyon and offers a good vantage point for photographers. The meadow, views of North Dome and the Grand Sentinel, the Kings River, and the surrounding forest all converge at the boardwalk, making this spot a fitting climax to the hike. Return to the junction with the River Trail and turn right to retrace your steps back over the suspension bridge to finish your hike.

Here's a warning to heed: warm summer evenings often bring out mosquitoes. Consider bringing some kind of insect repellent to keep these winged vampires at bay.

39 KANAWYERS LOOP

Distance: 4.6 miles (7.4 km)
Elevation gain: 300 feet (90 m)
High point: 5157 feet (1572 m)
Difficulty: Moderate
Trail surface: Dirt
Map: USGS 7.5-min The Sphinx
GPS: 36.794682°, -118.582809°
Notes: Day use only; good for kids; restroom at trailhead; permit station at trailhead

> Hiking in Kings Canyon is often a tale of two extremes: severe and exceedingly gentle. Many of the canyon's trails ascend precipitous canyon walls along exhausting switchbacks to remote high points. In stark contrast, many other canyon routes provide excellent scenery but little exertion. For hikers seeking a middle way, consider this looping route exploring the most beautiful part of Kings Canyon, which was named after an enterprising pioneer couple.

GETTING THERE

From Kings Canyon National Park's Big Stump Entrance, drive east for 1.7 miles (2.7 km) on CA Highway 180, and keep left at a junction with Generals Highway. Continue driving east for another 31 miles (49.9 km) into Cedar Grove. Continue beyond Cedar Grove for another 5.4 miles (8.7 km) to Roads End. A connector trail that leads to the River Trail departs from the south side of the Roads End parking loop.

ON THE TRAIL

From the Roads End parking area, follow a connector trail south to a steel footbridge crossing the South Fork Kings

A classic dry meadow scene on the Kanawyers Loop

River at 0.2 mile (0.4 km). The impossibly clear water rushes below the bridge, and the translucent green-and-blue hues of the water appear otherworldly. Contrasted against this turbulent scene, the towering ramparts of Kings Canyon's northern wall loom overhead in austere silence.

On the opposite side of the bridge, find the River Trail. Turn left, and continue through pine, cedar, and oak forest as the trail parallels the river. Soon after, the trail leaves the cover of the forest and enters a dry meadow that reveals spacious views east toward the confluence of Bubbs Creek Canyon and the South Fork Kings River—a spot you will reach about halfway through the loop.

Before you reach this confluence, you will have to negotiate an unimproved crossing of Avalanche Creek (2 miles/3.2 km). The creek swells with spring and early-summer snowmelt, and the crossing may require a lot of care and patience

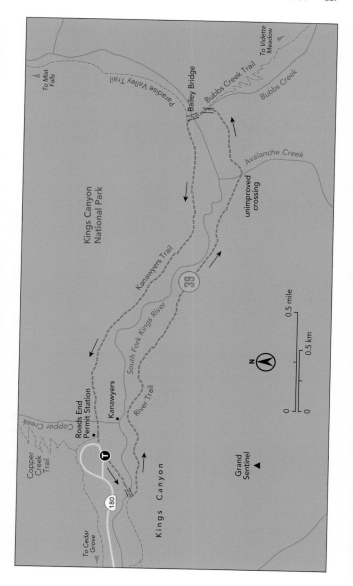

unless you're willing to take off your shoes and get wet. Even then, the water can flow swiftly. Trekking poles will help you to maintain your balance.

Beyond Avalanche Creek, the trail bends to the north to cross over a series of bridges spanning forks of Bubbs Creek (2.3 miles/3.7 km), which braids out during high water. Beyond the bridges, you arrive at a junction with the Bubbs Creek Trail at 2.4 miles (3.9 km) just before the banks of the main watercourse of Bubbs Creek. Turn left to follow the trail to the Bailey Bridge. On the other side of the bridge, you reach a junction with the Paradise Valley Trail leading to Mist Falls (2.5 miles/4 km). Keep left here to return to Roads End.

Just before you reach Roads End at 4.6 miles (7.4 km), walk south from the Copper Creek crossing east of Roads End along the eastern bank of the creek to reach the site of the Kanawyers resort. Today, it's nothing more than some vague ruins, but it was from this spot that the seeds of Kings Canyon National Park were sown.

NAP AND VIOLET KANAWYER

The name of the loop refers to Violet and Napoleon Kanawyer, a pair of failed copper miners who instead turned their energies toward catering to early Kings Canyon tourists. From their rudimentary resort located just east of present-day Roads End, the Kanawyers led intrepid early visitors deep into the Kings Canyon high country while opening the door for outdoor enthusiasts such as John Muir to begin singing the praises of a rival to Yosemite Valley. These praises, coupled with the photography of Ansel Adams, ultimately swayed Congress to incorporate the canyon into a new national park instead of allowing water companies to flood the canyon as a new reservoir.

40 MIST FALLS

Distance: 8 miles (12.9 km)
Elevation gain: 900 feet (270 m)
High point: 5857 feet (1785 m)
Difficulty: Challenging
Trail surface: Dirt and occasional granite outcrops
Map: USGS 7.5-min The Sphinx
GPS: 36.794682°, -118.582809°
Notes: Day use only to the falls, but suitable for backpacking at Lower Paradise Valley; restroom at trailhead; permit station at trailhead

Picture this: on a cool May morning before the sun crests the cliffs and peaks to the east, a bear shuffles past truck-sized boulders and the cinnamon-pillars of incense cedars. The bear sniffs here and there, constantly on the alert for something edible, as you keep your distance in the hopes that a sudden movement does not spook him deeper into the forest. The distant rumble of the South Fork Kings River drones on your right while the forest's birds begin their chorus of post-dawn chatter. Several memorable miles along the Kings River lay ahead of you as you follow the course of its stunning canyon to the Kings Canyon region's most beautiful waterfall.

GETTING THERE

From Kings Canyon National Park's Big Stump Entrance, drive east for 1.7 miles (2.7 km) on CA Highway 180, and keep left at a junction with Generals Highway. Continue driving east for another 31 miles (49.9 km) into Cedar Grove. Continue beyond Cedar Grove for another 5.4 miles (8.7 km) to Roads End. The trail to Mist Falls begins on the eastern edge of the parking area next to the Roads End Permit Station.

ON THE TRAIL

The initial segment of the trail to Mist Falls follows the Kanawyers Trail along the course of the Kings River from Roads End to the confluence of Bubbs Creek and the South Fork. This nearly flat segment passes through dense forest nurtured by the river alternating with drier, open ponderosa pine woodland with an understory of manzanita. Due east, a granitic spire known as the Sphinx stands high above the south wall. As you progress up the South Fork from the confluence, views of the Sphinx from various aspects provide an ongoing, evolving visual highlight.

Just after passing through a dense, marshy segment of trail that carries the highest likelihood of both a bear sighting and an airborne mosquito assault, you reach the Bubbs Creek Trail and the Bubbs Creek–South Fork confluence at 1.9 miles (3.1 km). Keep left to hike north along the South Fork Kings River as it cascades down a moderate slope over massive boulders. During peak run-off, the sight and the sound of the swollen river as it thunders down toward the confluence strike awe and perhaps even some trepidation. Impressive volumes of water can flow through this canyon, and even in late summer following a wet year, the cascades can be impressive.

As the trail settles into a moderate incline, continue through a series of different habitats common to Kings Canyon. Canyon live oaks intermingle with incense cedars, sugar pines, ponderosa pines, and deciduous black oaks. Deciduous black cottonwoods crowd the banks of the river where the flow is not so swift as to uproot any tree that attempts to establish a foothold. Interspersed between long stretches of the forested west bank of the river lie several granite outcrops. At these outcrops, the forest cover clears to offer spectacular views down canyon toward the Sphinx, which rises above two pronounced avalanche chutes.

The pristine blue-green waters of the Kings River

The canyon widens perceptibly just before reaching the base of Mist Falls at 4 miles (6.4 km). Here, the river pours into a broad, semicircular amphitheater. A social trail will lead you close to the falls, but the heavy mist and dangerously slick rocks will repel most people who want to get close. In addition to the sometimes copious water vapor, the river remains swift and treacherous even into the summer when snowmelt diminishes. Several logs or clearings well back from the chilly mist provide ideal spots to rest and picnic before turning around or continuing on.

GOING FARTHER

If you wish to continue beyond Mist Falls to Paradise Valley, return to the trail and continue the uphill climb heading

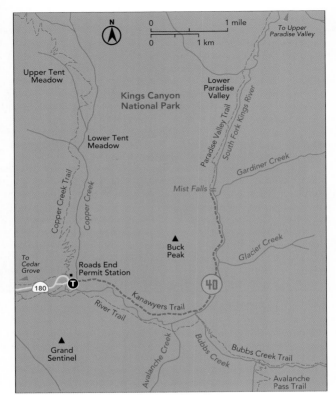

up-canyon. After an additional 1.4 miles (2.3 km) of hiking that gain another 750 feet (230 km) of elevation, you reach the mouth of Paradise Valley. The canyon floor flattens out, allowing the Kings River to meander placidly. Continue for another 0.4 mile (0.6 km) to find the campsites for Lower Paradise Valley. This is the first place where camping is allowed along the route. Further campsites lie upstream at Middle Paradise Valley (8.3 miles/13.4 km) and Upper Paradise Valley (9.7 miles/15.6 km).

ACKNOWLEDGMENTS

Thanks to all of the friends who joined me on trips to the sequoias, including Tony Cohen, Kevin Jontz, Sean Matthes, Taylor Corbin, and Kyle Kuns. Thank you in particular to my wife, Kelly, for always being so supportive of my trips into the wilderness and my guidebooking endeavors. Thanks to Kate Rogers for giving me the opportunity to turn what has been a long-standing passion project into this fantastic little guidebook. Thanks to all of the Mountaineers Books staff, including Erin Cusick, Heidi Smets, Erin Greb, and Janet Kimball, for their help in bringing this book to life. And finally, thank you to all of the dedicated staff at Sequoia and Kings Canyon National Parks, not just for answering my questions and helping to make sure I got things right, but for tirelessly fighting to protect one of the most beautiful places on our planet.

APPENDIX A: AGENCY CONTACT INFORMATION

Cedar Grove Visitor Center
North Side Drive (next to Sentinel
Campground)
559-565-3793
Open mid-May to mid-October;
daily from 9:00 AM to 5:00 PM.

Foothills Visitor Center
47050 Generals Highway
Three Rivers, CA 93271
559-565-3341
Open daily from 8:00 AM to
4:30 PM. Hours vary in winter.

Giant Forest Museum
On Generals Highway, 16.4 miles
(26.4 km) from the Ash Mountain
Entrance.
559-565-3341
Open daily from 9:00 AM to
4:30 PM. Hours vary in winter.

Kings Canyon Visitor Center
83918 CA Highway 180
Kings Canyon National Park,
CA 93633
559-565-3341
Open daily from 8:00 AM to 5:00 PM.
Hours vary according to season.

Lodgepole Visitor Center
63100 Lodgepole Road
Sequoia National Park, CA 93262
559-565-4436
Hours vary according to season.

Mineral King Ranger Station
Mile 24, Mineral King Road
Three Rivers, CA 93271
559-565-3768
Open seasonally (late spring to
mid-fall, depending on snow),
8:00 AM to 4:00 PM

Roads End Ranger Station
Located at the end of
CA Highway 180
559-565-3341
Open mid-May to mid-October;
daily from 7:00 AM to 3:00 PM

**Sequoia and Kings Canyon
National Park Headquarters**
47050 Generals Highway
Three Rivers, CA 93271-9700
559-565-3341
Phone calls only; leave message or
dial 1 for current weather, road, and
fire conditions.

Sequoia Parks Conservancy
47050 Generals Highway Unit 10
Three Rivers, CA 93271
559-561-4813
Visit www.sequoiaparksconservancy
.org for information on their work
and how to support it.

OPPOSITE: *Foxtail pines live up to three thousand years.*

APPENDIX B: RECOMMENDED READING

GEOLOGY

Alt, David D., and Donald W. Hyndman. *Roadside Geology of Northern and Central California*. Missoula, MT: Mountain Press Publishing Company, 2016.

Hill, Mary. *Geology of the Sierra Nevada*. Berkeley: University of California Press, 2006.

NATURAL HISTORY

Howell, Catherine H. *Reptiles and Amphibians of North America*. Des Moines, IA: National Geographic Books, 2015.

Jameson, Everett W., and Hans J. Peeters. *Mammals of California*. Berkeley: University of California Press, 2004.

Little, Elbert. *National Audubon Society Field Guide to North American Trees: Western Region*. New York: Alfred A. Knopf, 1980.

Sibley, David A. *The Sibley Guide to Birds*. 2nd ed. New York: Alfred A. Knopf, 2014.

Storer, Tracy I., Robert L. Usinger, and David Lukas. *Sierra Nevada Natural History*. Berkeley: University of California Press, 2004.

Wiese, Karen. *Sierra Nevada Wildflowers*. Helena, MT: Falcon Guides, 2013.

HISTORY

Jackson, Louise. *The Sierra Nevada Before History: Ancient Landscapes, Early Peoples*. Missoula, MT: Mountain Press Publishing Company, 2010.

Tweed, William C., and Lary M. Dilsaver. *Challenge of the Big Trees*. Three Rivers, CA: Sequoia Parks Foundation, 2016.

Tweed, William C. *Uncertain Path: A Search for the Future of National Parks*. Berkeley, CA: University of California Press, 2011.

MISCELLANEOUS

Burns, Bob, and Mike Burns. *Wilderness Navigation: Finding Your Way Using Map, Compass, Altimeter, and GPS*. Seattle: Mountaineers Books, 2015.

INDEX

ABOUT THE AUTHOR

Scott Turner is a native-Californian hiking-guide author who moonlights as a marriage and family therapist. When he isn't helping families and individuals through mental health challenges, he's attempting to shrink an ever-expanding bucket list of journeys and explorations of the American West's most beautiful places.  He's the author of *Hike the Parks: Joshua Tree National Park* and *Hike the Parks: Zion & Bryce Canyon National Parks,* both from Mountaineers Books. Other writing credits include a revision and update of Jerry Schad's "hiking Bible" for San Diego, *Afoot & Afield: San Diego County,* and over 250 descriptions of trails across Southern California, the Sierra Nevada, Hawaii, Utah, Arizona, and Montana for Modern Hiker, the West Coast's most widely read hiking website. Scott lives in sunny Carlsbad, California, with his wife, Kelly, his son, Hank, and his cat, Dingleberry.

MOUNTAINEERS BOOKS, including its two imprints, Skipstone and Braided River, is a leading publisher of quality outdoor recreation, sustainability, and conservation titles. As a 501(c)(3) nonprofit, we are committed to supporting the environmental and educational goals of our organization by providing expert information on human-powered adventure, sustainable practices at home and on the trail, and preservation of wilderness.

Our publications are made possible through the generosity of donors, and through sales of more than 700 titles on outdoor recreation, sustainable lifestyle, and conservation. To donate, purchase books, or learn more, visit us online:

MOUNTAINEERS BOOKS
1001 SW Klickitat Way, Suite 201 • Seattle, WA 98134 • 800-553-4453
mbooks@mountaineersbooks.org • www.mountaineersbooks.org

An independent nonprofit publisher since 1960

Leave No Trace strives to educate visitors about the nature of their recreational impacts and offers techniques to prevent and minimize such impacts. Leave No Trace is best understood as an educational and ethical program, not as a set of rules and regulations. For more information, visit www.lnt.org or call 800-332-4100.

YOU MAY ALSO LIKE

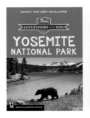